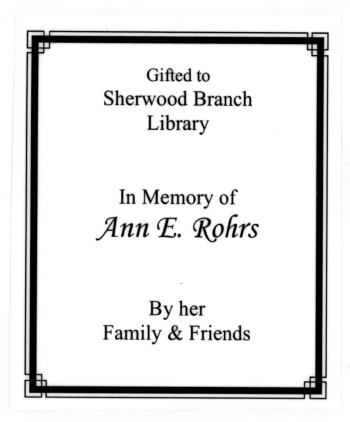

Gifted to
Sherwood Branch
Library

In Memory of
Ann E. Rohrs

By her
Family & Friends

HE STARTED THE WHOLE WORLD SINGING

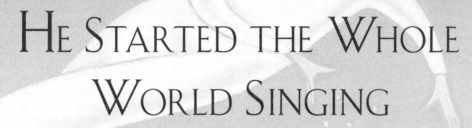

HE STARTED THE WHOLE WORLD SINGING

A Treasury of Gaither Christmas Songs,
Reflections, and Holiday Traditions

GLORIA GAITHER

WARNER
Faith
NEW YORK BOSTON NASHVILLE

Scriptures noted THE MESSAGE are taken from *The Message: The New Testament in Contemporary English.* Copyright © 1993 by Eugene H. Peterson. • Scriptures noted TLB are taken from *The Living Bible,* copyright © 1971. Used by permission of Tyndale House Publishers, Inc., Wheaton, Illinois 60189. All rights reserved. • Scriptures noted KJV are taken from the King James Version of the Bible. • Scriptures noted NEB are taken from *The New English Bible with the Apocrypha,* copyright © 1961, 1970, 1989 by Oxford University Press, Inc., and Cambridge University Press, Inc. Used by permission of Oxford University Press, Inc. • Scriptures noted NIV are taken from *The Holy Bible: New International Version®.* Copyright © 1973, 1978, 1984 by International Bible Society. Used by permission of Zondervan Publishing House. All rights reserved. • Scriptures noted NKJV are taken from the *New King James Version.* Copyright © 1979, 1980, 1982, Thomas Nelson, Inc., Publishers.

Warner Faith
Time Warner Book Group
1271 Avenue of the Americas, New York, NY 10020

Visit our Web site at www.twbookmark.com.

Warner Faith® and the Warner Faith logo are trademarks of Time Warner Book Group Inc.

Book design by Fearn Cutler de Vicq
Printed in the United States of America

First Warner Books printing: October 2004
10 9 8 7 6 5 4 3 2

Library of Congress Cataloging-in-Publication Data

Gaither, Gloria.
    He started the whole world singing : a treasury of Gaither Christmas songs, reflections, and holiday traditions / Gloria Gaither.—1st Warner Books Printing.
        p. cm.
        ISBN 0-446-53367-x
    1. Gaither, Gloria. 2. Gaither, Bill. 3. Gospel musicians—United States—Biography.
        I. Gaither, Gloria. Songs. Texts. Selections. II. Title.
    ML420. G13A3 2004

    782.25'4'0922—dc22   2004008291

Dedicated to Flaxy Floyd Mahoney Sickal,

who made Christmas a wonderland for me, and who, at the age of sixty-something,

gave herself the gift of a name she'd always loved—so she could die "Alice."

CONTENTS

vii

ACKNOWLEDGMENTS

Although I have actually put the words of this book on paper, all the songs and all my life have been shared with Bill, my sweet "companion of the road." I may be the words, but he is the tune in more ways than just songs. I want to thank him, most of all, for encouraging me to write, and for loving me while I do.

Thanks, too, to our three children, who have always given us plenty to write about as we have lived out our calling together as a family; and we are thankful for the amazing gift of a new generation—now five—who make us laugh, play, sing, and give thanks every day of our lives.

Deep appreciation for Teri Garner, my assistant, who keeps my life in some kind of order, and to my wonderful editor, Steve Wilburn, who brings such a wide and rich perspective from our wild brainstorming sessions to the finished product.

Gratitude, too, to the women of the Monday morning prayer group, who keep my confidences, pray like the house is on fire, and believe I can when all evidence may be to the contrary.

Clarifying light
For whom the story told if not for me;
For whom the storyteller if not for you, Yahweh?

—Ann Johnson, *Miryam of Nazareth*

WORDS FROM THE AUTHOR

Christmas (the Mass of Christ) is a holy celebration of the most holy event in the history of the world. This God whose holiness forbade even the utterance of His name, this awesome Creator, chose to invade our planet in this galaxy so that we could, at last, not only say His name but experience His true nature after centuries of misunderstanding and partial information.

The theology of Christmas is at once centrally vital, yet beyond our ability to make it "systematic." Heaven and earth in one zygote. God and a human woman joined without physical contact. Limitless eternity limited to a thirty-three-year life lived by a man in a Middle Eastern town with no place to call home. The Word— that vibrating sound wave, common denominator of all matter, that bombastic Word that *was* the "big bang" and continues to speak order out of chaos, that total Truth and Love and Energy—was reduced to a whimper from a manger. The Bread of Life sprouts in a dish for animals' grain in a town whose name means "city of bread." Who can wrap a mind around it all?

Yet, it is not only the transcendence of it that amazes us. It is the detailed, common, simple, painful, beautiful humanity of it all: the peasant status, the unceremonial circumstances, the rustic setting, and the lack of privilege.

We know that we are called, as Ann Johnson says in *Miryam of Nazareth* (Ave Maria Press, 1984), to a spirituality that transcends our humanity. But could it be that we are, as she suggests, also called to a humanity that transcends our spirituality—"a humanity so simply lived that we do not practice spiritual rigors to condition ourselves for closeness to God"? Rather, could we be called to a humanity "so filled with the love of God/neighbor that the Word is commonly spoken in simple miracles of God-bearing, healing, sharing . . . spoken in song and dance, in loving remembrances of those who have gone before and in rejoicing embraces of those we talk with, feed, nurture and with whom we celebrate"?

In my experience, God more often comes in surprising, daily, unglamorous, and un-pious ways. The liturgy that chants its way into my Monday mornings is, more often than otherwise, uttered not by priests and clergy, but by children who have no idea of what wonder they are inspiring. The incense that wafts its way above my head like the fragrance of the Holy Spirit is the aroma of forgiveness I haven't had the good sense to ask for, or the sweet perfume of a spontaneous embrace when words won't come and won't do.

As I think back over my life, the high moments of ministry have come in the form of a cool washcloth on my forehead when I was vomiting or a call from someone who knew the weight of my load, offering a pot of hot soup for the family supper or an afternoon of childcare so I could get groceries without hauling toddlers in and out of car seats. A few times, it's just been someone offering to sew on a button or fix a torn hem at the last minute so I could get on stage.

I think we sometimes forget in spiritualizing the glory of Christmas that this Bethlehem story is one of sore backs, sore feet, labor pains, desperation, and inconvenience. It is the story of a soon-to-be husband's patient endurance, a harried innkeeper's considerate offer when there was no room or reservation, and an inexperienced girl giving birth without necessary provisions (and without her mother around).

And lest we get too romantic about the whole scenario, it was not the frightened mother who heard the confirming angels, but some nomadic flock-followers who had no idea what the commotion was all about. It was not the patient and worn-out Joseph who was inspired by the star to keep going, but some shy scholar who had no real tie to this most human development in Bethlehem.

Stories are told in their entirety only in hindsight. As Marcel Proust believed, memory may actually be the only truth. Only in memory do we know what came before an event and what followed it. While things are happening, each person is living out only his or her own seemingly isolated piece of the puzzle. This has been true of my life: not at all spiritual, inspiring, or full of wonder while it's happening.

Today's Christmases are very similar in many ways to the first. We don't know how profound the details are while they're happening. For example, I could never have anticipated how intensely personal the story of the Incarnation was going to become until I was pregnant with my first baby. But when the labor pains started in earnest on December 15, and I was alone at home, scrubbing down the walls of our little house because the furnace had belched smoke onto the yellow paint, I felt a bit of the panic Mary must have felt when she feared her baby would come before she could find a safe place to have Him. On that Christmas Eve, still sore and faint from a hard delivery and loss of blood, I held our little dark-haired child while someone read the Christmas story in our family circle. "And she brought forth her firstborn son, and wrapped him in swaddling clothes . . ." (Luke 2:7 KJV), the story went. But in my mind I was thinking, *How did she ever ride that donkey back to Nazareth?*

How could we have known a few Christmas Eves ago that the pictures we took of us piled around Bill's mother on the couch, holding the newest babies and fussing over the children, would not be developed until after her funeral. Would we have sung any sweeter than we did that night when our son, Benjy, for some unknown reason, brought his guitar? Would we have laughed with more joy at the little ones' requesting not only "Jingle Bells" and "Rudolph" but also "Twist and Shout" and Nanci Griffith hits?

I remember like it was yesterday finding a layaway slip in my father's billfold for something he'd been making payments on for Christmas. He had died in his sleep the night we were singing in Kansas City. We thought he had a cold because he'd been coughing so hard, but as it turned out, the congestion was in his heart cavity and not his lungs. After the funeral it fell on me to visit the jewelry store to see what he'd been buying for Christmas.

The diamond cluster the lady brought out to me had a story of its own. My parents were converted in a very strict holiness church, and trying to follow God, Mother was convinced her wedding rings were "worldly" and she sold them. After a while Daddy was called to preach, and from then on we never had enough money for Mother to have expensive jewelry. We were lucky to have money left on Sunday night for a family trip to Dairy Queen. (Daddy didn't get paid until Monday.)

Daddy had always been sad that Mother had sold her rings, though she never complained. As soon as I saw the ring that day in December, I knew Daddy was going to put these diamonds on the finger of his bride if it was the last thing he ever did. It was. Only he didn't get to see them there.

Like the first Christmas, our Christmases have puzzle pieces as profound as shepherds, mangers, and the tax census. Only we usually don't know until the puzzle is finished; the details seem unrelated until the whole story is written. Pieced together, they make the mosaic of Christmas holy.

If those events in Nazareth and Bethlehem taught us anything, it must be that God came to blur the line between the mundane and the divine. He came to let us know that this great and awesome Jehovah intended from the beginning that our regular days be so filled with awe and wonder that we really couldn't bear any more miracles. Just the unspoiled trust of a young girl or the birth of a baby or the compassion and sensitivity of strangers are marvels enough! Maybe He came to peel the glaze off our faded eyes so that we recognize a star-studded night when we see one and can pick out the singing of angels from the lowing of oxen, the bleating of sheep, and the children arguing on the hillside.

"Immanuel." Yes. God is with us. As architect Mies van der Rohe said, "God *is* in the details." But too often we bludgeon the details with our stampeding feet, racing off to some new, more indulgent deity—one that will give us money instead of riches, "perks" instead of treasure, parties instead of peace.

I pray that this is the season we, like the shepherds, will recognize something amazingly angelic in the voices of our own children. It is my hope that the "Incarnation story" will be written with the details of our own scenarios, personal experiences in which God *does* come to dwell in us, in our human gatherings and our make-do celebrations, even if we end up having Christmas in the barn because it's the only place big enough to accommodate all of us.

And may some of us this year see the star, know that this is no ordinary event, and bring to the party lavish, extravagant gifts of forgiveness, mercy, and grace that will sustain the ones who need to travel to a new heart place where hateful pursuers cannot harm the spirit.

May the sky explode above all our heads with unstoppable music that cannot be stifled by wars, taxes, or dull routine. Glory in the Highest, indeed!

Advent Prayer

It is advent. I am waiting—waiting for Your coming, Lord.

There are so many places where I wait for Your coming.

You came to Bethlehem, that tiny place of an almost forgotten promise.

You came to Nazareth, no spectacular town,
> and You came to Bethany, Capernaum, and Jerusalem.

There are places in my life that await Your coming.

Here—where Your message of reconciliation is so needed;
> or there—where Your tears could fall as they did over Jerusalem.

I need You to come where it would take at least a choir of angels
> to make the dullest of hearts aware of something eternal.

I wait for Your entrance into those dark places of disbelief—
> the crude and mundane corners of my existence so in need of starlight
> illuminations.

Come where there is little privacy, comfort, or warmth—
> where animals feed and lowly service is offered.

How many times have I plunged headlong into the celebration of Your coming
> without being assured of Your actual arrival?

I have gone more days than three "assuming You to be in our presence."
But Advent is not for scurrying or for assuming.

  It is for waiting.
May I recognize You when You come

  not as the peak moment of our preplanned celebration,

    but as the subtle surprise,

      the simple object of wonder,

        the God of small things.
I wait. Come, Lord Jesus, come.

The Songs

Bring Back the Glory

All the laughter is gone,
And the sound of the song
That we sang slowly faded away.
Simple joys that we knew
When we walked close to You
Hand in hand in the cool of the day.
Joys are just memories.
Or are they dreams?
Yet, we hold to the hope
That the music will come back again.

Bring back the glory.
Won't You show us what life is for?
Bring back the glory.
Make us open once more.
Bring back the music, the trust,
The wonder that's just

Like a child who has never known pain.
Bring back the glory,
Bring back the glory,
Bring back the glory,
And put us together again!

With our innocence gone,
How the days linger on
While we keep all our laws and decrees.
Even when we do right,
There's no song in the night,
There's no love, there's no joy, there's no peace.
And yet, somehow,
We don't know how,
There's a longing that says to us
Life must be more than just bread.

There's no cause that is grand,
There's no vision to stand for
That calls for the best we can see.
Nothing worthy to live for,

3

No reason to give everything
That we ever could be.
There must be more.
What are we for?
How we need You to give us
A glimpse of eternity.

   You are the Glory!
   You have shown us what life is for.
   You are the Glory!
   Make us like You once more!
   You are the Music, the Trust, the
         Wonder that's just like a child
           Who has never known pain.
   You are the Glory!
   You are the Glory!
   The Glory that brings us
   Together again!

Lyric: Gloria Gaither
Music: William J. Gaither and Bill George

Bring Back the Glory

In the very beginning, all creation was full of the glory of the Lord. All living things worked together in harmony, the harmony that comes from knowing life is eternal and every moment is a part of forever. There was beauty; there was trust. Dreams were not a fantasy but an everyday reality, and music filled the air with the song of the free.

This glory and splendor flooded everything with the shining light of openness, for where there is glory there is no fear, no suspicion, and no guilt. Because man and woman knew the glory, they stood straight and tall, comfortable with each other, with nature, and with their God.

There was no need for status or competition. There was only the deep awareness of the infinite value of each living creature. Work was a joy, union with each other was a celebration, and encounter with God's holiness was as natural and as beautiful as the sight of the first rays of a new dawn.

But the Lord of Glory was not the only presence there. The Prince of Darkness lurked there, too, and he could not bear the glory. God's purity had longed for communion, but Evil wanted company in his cynicism and guile. So, true to his deceptive nature, he used man's very innocence and a twisted half-truth to lure him into selling wisdom for knowledge, forfeiting fulfillment for indulgence, and trading contentment for cheap thrills.

So man and woman broke away from the embrace of Love . . . and the glory departed. Life lost its joy. Work became a chore. Parenting came to know pain. There was no song, and the days passed without a dream. The people began to wander in search of something that had become only a dim memory, a fading shadow in the corridors of their minds.

Yet, although they had lost the glory, the hungry vacuum that remained in its place would not let them go. There was a deep knowing: *There must be more.* They called to God for answers, and God answered with a promise: *One day the glory will return.*

But God needed a people who would obey Him, who would trust in Him alone, a people who would keep the memory of His promise alive and would not be tricked again by the voices who called themselves gods and promised easy answers.

God needed a courageous people who would dare to stand alone when others did not believe. He needed a people who were willing, by their discipline and obedience, to save the frame that would one day hold the promised Glory.

God called His people Zion. Zion—the people of God. Yes, He called them out and caused them to rebuild their lives with worn-out tools and broken dreams on the rubble that once had been perfection. He gave them His instructions. So, with the fragments of remembered glory, they built traditions and ceremonies, shaped systems and governments, and hammered out restrictions and rules.

Time and again, they were pursued and enslaved by those who didn't share their dream and who thought the promise of hope was a joke. Yet, in all the years of bondage, they could never forget *they had a birthright.* Though they wandered far from home, they could never wander beyond the sound of a higher calling.

God had promised to make a way to bring His creation back to Himself, and though there were many Babylons along the way, Zion kept calling through their tears. Yes, tears flowed like wine, for there is no grief so bitter as the mourning over departed glory. They called to their God; they grieved for their children who had never known the glory of life.

> Let me alone to weep. Don't try to comfort me—let me cry for my people . . . My people have given up their glorious God for silly idols! . . . They have forsaken me, the Fountain of Life-giving Water: and they have built for themselves broken cisterns . . . They exchanged the glory of God for the disgrace of idols . . . All your waves and billows have gone over me, and floods of sorrow pour upon me like a thundering cataract. Yet day by day the Lord also pours out his steadfast love upon me, and through the night I sing his songs and pray to God who gives me life. (Isaiah 22:4; Jeremiah 2:11, 13; Hosea 4:7; Psalm 42:7–8 TLB)

Although they had left the glory, God did not abandon them but kept wooing them with His promise that one day He would make a way. He promised to turn their sorrow into joy and their weeping into music. There were some who listened for the voice of God and believed in hope.

Yes, God's people—those who had chosen to obey Him in faith—believed the promise. They met together to encourage one another to go on hoping even when times were hard. As they shared the symbols of God's faithfulness to them, they would always say: "Next year in Jerusalem." By this they meant that one day they would be brought back together in a place where they could belong.

The glory would return and they would once more know oneness with each other, with nature, and with their God. The broken segments of their lives and the broken chords of their songs would be restored, and the tears would be no more.

Lord, you have poured out amazing blessings on this land! . . . Now bring us back to loving you, O Lord, so that your anger will never need rise against us again . . .

Pour out your love and kindness on us, Lord, and grant us your salvation. I am listening carefully to all the Lord is saying—for he speaks peace to his people, if they will only stop their sinning. Surely his salvation is near to those who reverence him; our land will be filled with his glory . . . The wise shall inherit *glory*. (Psalm 85:1–4, 7–9 TLB; Proverbs 3:35 KJV, emphasis added)

But some were not wise. They forgot the promise and scoffed at those who believed. They called them *dreamers*. Yet there were those who could not forget, and these cried out to God with a growing urgency. Even when times were hard and faith was costly, they held to their hope and prayed that the glory would return.

Open up, O ancient gates, and let the King of Glory in!
Who is the King of Glory?
Yes, open wide the gates and let the King of Glory in!
Who is the King of Glory?

"From the uttermost part of the earth have we heard songs, even glory to the righteous" (Isaiah 24:16 KJV).

Through the years, they must have asked, "Who is this King, this One who will bring glory back to this land? When will the singing be heard once more, and who will be the Song?"

The years of waiting were long and hard. Those who believed the promise were often persecuted and ridiculed and driven from their homes. The sound of hope sometimes grew dim in their ears, and they were no strangers to doubt.

But hope did come! It broke like the dawn onto a dark, lonely hillside, in a song so glorious it could not be denied by even the dullest of ears.

Yes! The Song was Jesus, and in Him, God kept His promise. It was not just a carol that burst into that first Christmas night; it was the Source of all music—born; it was the living Word made flesh; it was the promised Glory—returned!

He Started the Whole World Singing

Before the song started, the world brokenhearted,
Was dreamlessly passing the long, empty days;
Then a dark, lonely hillside was spangled with light,
And a song burst into the night!

A new Word was spoken, and chords that were broken
Wove gently together to make a new song.
It was more than a carol to greet the new morn
For the Source of all music was born!

He started the whole world singing a song.
The words and the music were there all along!
What the song had to say was that Love found a way
To start the world singing a song!

Lyric: Gloria Gaither
Music: William J. Gaither and Chris Waters

❧❧❧ *He Started the Whole World Singing*

New York at Christmas is unlike any other place on earth—a candy store for the senses. Already uniquely diverse and stimulating, at Christmastime the city assaults you with lights, smells, and sounds at every turn. Hot dog vendors, pretzel makers, and chestnut roasters send aromas into the chilly air. Speakers flood the street with music from the doorway of every restaurant and store. The sides of skyscrapers illuminate the skyline with symbols of the season painted in colored lights. The designer-arranged store windows of huge department stores are so amazing that people line up to take pictures of them.

At Rockefeller Center, the world-famous Christmas tree, sparkling with thousands of lights and ornaments, towers over the skaters who glide across the ice-covered square flanked by enormous golden angels.

A horse-drawn-carriage ride at night through Central Park with someone you love is magical enough, but should the snow start to fall while you're wrapped cozy and warm in coats and lap blankets, you have the chance to experience one of the most romantic hours of your life.

Because our anniversary falls on December 22, Bill and I have celebrated a few times in New York. We love to eat in our favorite restaurants uninterrupted by phones, and then take in a great play or musical. Afterward, we walk around

Manhattan and Times Square, just like a couple of kids from some small country town in the Midwest—which we are.

One night at Christmas, we were eating in the grand old German restaurant called Luchow's. The place was decorated with ancient ornaments and garlands that looked as if they had actually come from Germany years before and had been some family's treasure.

An aging polka band played there then, and people who knew how got up to dance the polka. But it was Christmas, so the band played Christmas carols to people's requests and as they played, guests began to sing along. We couldn't help but join in. There we were, in the middle of a city with a reputation for being secular and politically correct, singing with folks we'd never met: "Joy to the world, the Lord has come! Let earth receive her King…"

One after another, those dining requested their favorites, and around these well-worn songs, instant community was created. People grinned at each other as the parts were added, and sometimes applauded when the song was over.

After the singing subsided and the band went back to playing traditional German pieces, Bill looked at me and said, "Well, at least He got everyone singing, didn't He?"

The next night, we had tickets to the Radio City Music Hall Christmas show. This is always an incredible production, and the performance was spectacular—from the Sugar Plum Fairy to Frosty the Snowman and Rudolph the Red-nosed Reindeer, everything to delight a child appeared bigger than life. The dramatization of

Virginia's letter to Santa and the classic "Yes, Virginia, there is a Santa Claus" letter returned to her from the *New York Times* left even the hardest of hearts wishing every child had someone to be Santa for them.

The precision choreography of the famous Rockettes, dancing the "March of the Toy Soldiers," brought the entire audience to its feet in thunderous applause. Then the curtain closed, and a whole different atmosphere was created. A strong voice began to read the Christmas story from the second chapter of Luke. When the curtain reopened, the huge stage was a craggy hillside, and the characters in the true story of Christmas began to enter the scene: Mary and Joseph, the infant Jesus, shepherds with their sheep and goats; animals that belonged in the stable and the donkey that had made the trip to Bethlehem all came to the hilltop shelter. Along the side of the great auditorium came the camels, too, and the Oriental kings in lavish array, bowing at last before the baby Monarch and offering gifts to honor His birth.

Then a screen fell slowly and on it, scrolling down line-by-line, was the wonderful piece we have come to know as "One Solitary Life."

Awe and wonder reduced the audience to total silence at the panorama before us. No one moved as the voice finished the last lines:

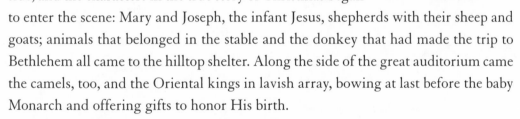

Of all the armies that ever marched,
all the navies that were ever built;
all the parliaments that ever sat
and all the kings that ever reigned, put together,
have not affected the life of man upon this earth
as powerfully as that one solitary life.

(From James Allan Francis, *The Real Jesus; and Other Sermon*s [Philadelphia: Judson, 1926])

The silence remained.

When Bill and I got home, we talked about the song of Jesus, how His coming to earth gave us back the song that had been silent so long through the centuries. He began writing the music for the chorus to "He Started the Whole World Singing," and a few months later, we began writing a musical that was born of these experiences. I began to explore the biblical story of the departing and return of the glory that was present in the beginning when man and God walked together and found delight in each other.

I discovered that the quaint old word *glory* means the "eternal" that infused everything—all of life—before sin entered the picture. And during those long years after the glory departed and the song died, God chose a people and gave them the promise that one day the glory would return and life would have a song. He gave them the law as a gift to "save the frame" for the promised glory; and He instructed

His people to keep the story alive, until God's plan would be made perfect again, by telling their children of when God walked and talked with man and woman.

No wonder the angels sang that night to the shepherds: "Glory! Gloria to the highest degree! This night is born to you a Savior which is Christ the Lord!" What they sang that night was not *a* song; it was *the Song*. The song had returned to the world. The song had returned to their lives! And all over the world to this day the song goes on. The eternal has infused our days. The glory has returned to our lives. And the song still echoes in the hearts of those who allow it to invade their lives— even in the streets of New York.

❧❧❧ *I Saw Him in the Drugstore*

I saw him in the drugstore. He was a big, awkward-looking guy with work-worn hands. And he was at the card rack fumbling through the section marked BIRTHDAY—WIFE. I watched him as he picked one or two cards and read them and put them back. And I could tell by the look on his face he wasn't finding what he had in mind at all.

He read another card and put it back; picked another one, and finally he chose one of those corny-looking cards with flowers on the front. It probably said "Roses are red, violets are blue…" or something like that, and I could tell that he still wasn't happy with what he'd found.

Finally, he sighed and took the card to the checkout counter. He paid the lady; she put it in a brown paper sack, and he walked out the door. I suppose he took it home and scrawled something simple on the bottom of it like "Love, Pete," and he gave it to her. But it didn't say what he wanted it to say, because it just isn't easy to say the things that really matter. It isn't easy to say, "I really love you." Sometimes it's hard to say, "I'm sorry I was wrong." Sometimes it's hard to say, "I acted like a fool yesterday—please forgive me." Sometimes it just isn't easy to say, "You're the glue that holds my whole world together, and I think sometimes if it weren't for you, I'd just fall apart."

But, you know, I think she knew. I think by the way he put an awkward arm around her shoulder or kind of punched her on the elbow, she probably knew. And I think he knew that she'd know, because there's something about living with someone for a long time and having them right where you can kind of look them in the eye—those things that are so hard to say don't *have* to be said. Love says it.

I think God tried all down through history to tell us what He wanted us to know. He sent His prophets and His teachers, and they tried. And we got part of it. We got the part about God's justice, and His law. We got the part about when we do bad things, we somehow have to pay, but the part that God really wanted us to know—the part that says, "I really love you!"—we weren't getting that. God seemed so far away.

But before time began, God had a plan. He said, "I know what I'll do. I'll send My love right down there where they are, where they can see it and touch it and know it, and I'll send it as a little tiny, vulnerable baby so they'll *have* to touch it, and they'll *have* to hold it close." God's love—right where we are.

My Bible says, "The Word was made flesh, and dwelt among us, and we beheld his glory, the glory as of the only begotten of the Father, full of grace and truth" (John 1:14 KJV).

The story of Christmas has been told in a lot of ways. Prophets predicted that one day a deliverer, the offspring of King David, would come. But how like God, to send an ordinary baby. How like God, to choose to limit Himself to a body like ours, and one of our languages, and our time and space. How like God, when we were so broken and guilty, to choose to walk with us and touch us and make us whole.

And, how like God to reach beyond our questions and doubts, right past the exercises of our minds, on past our suspicions and cynicisms—all the way to where we are.

And so this great Creator
Who'd been reaching all along,
This God who formed the worlds
With His own hands,
Made Love become a Baby,
One of our very own,
And spoke His Word
So we could understand.

17

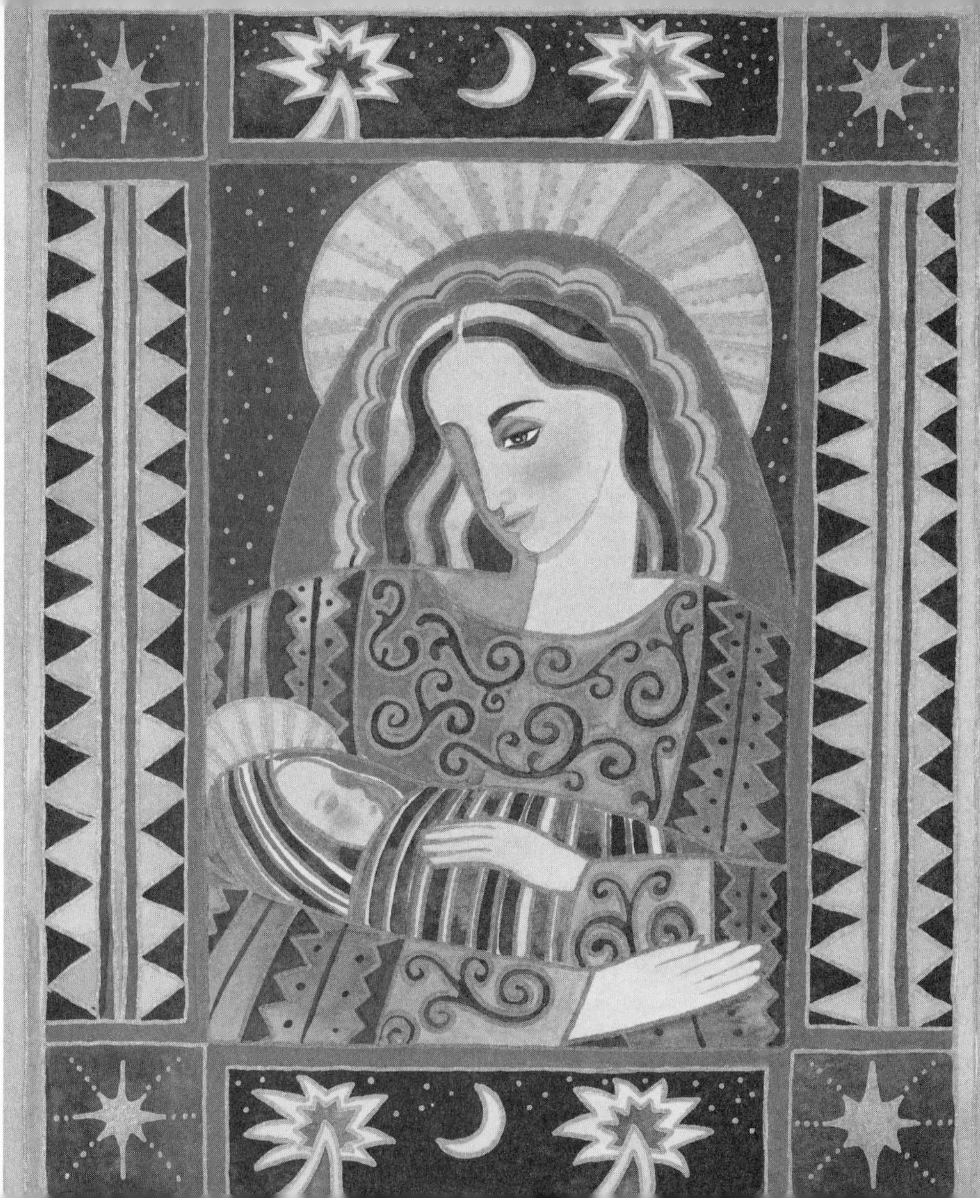

His Love . . . Reaching

Love has always been here,
In the chaos of our world,
It was the Word that echoed through the formless void;
And whether in the universe or worlds of our own minds,
It's love that turns our chaos into joy.

His love went on longing,
And His love went on reaching
Right past the shackles of my mind,
And the Word of the Father became Mary's little Son,
And His love reached all the way to where I was.

The Word that formed creation,
Man just couldn't understand;
Its sound was muffled by his wars and strifes.
And man destroyed resources
God intended just to be

The lovely backdrop for abundant life.

And so this great Creator
Who'd been reaching all along,
This God who formed the worlds
With His own hands,
Made Love become a Baby,
One of our very own,
And spoke His Word
So we could understand.

Lyric: Gloria Gaither
Music: William J. Gaither
Copyright © 1963 by Gaither Music Company.

20

❧❧❧ *His Love . . . Reaching*

Before anything else existed, there was Christ, with God. He has always been alive and is himself God. He created everything there is—nothing exists that he didn't make. (John 1:1–3 TLB)

All that came to be was alive with his life, and that life was the light of men. (John 1:4 NEB)

The coming of the Babe in the manger was not the first time Christ entered the world. He had always been there—with the Father, and the story of His love reaching out to man began as long ago as time itself.

At first, God's love reached out in creation, and His reaching had such enormous power that the firmament burst forth from His fingertips. The sun and moon took their places, and God sprinkled the night with a thousand stars. The waters found their way to their own boundaries, and the tides were forever set. Fish and creatures of the deep found their paths in the sea.

And God went on reaching, and dry land appeared; buds burst forth. Then came fields and grasses, hills and plains. Heartbeats of animals and all living creatures throbbed at the touch of God's reaching.

Even yet, Love, longing for someone to whom to give Himself, was not satisfied, for love needs someone to receive. So God reached farther and made a man.

But man did not understand. He took for granted the marvelous order and beauty that surrounded him. He didn't see that all the things God's love had created were a result of God's reaching out to him. Instead of returning God's love in gratitude by treasuring nature's resources, man selfishly used, wasted, and prostituted creation, blindly failing to recognize that it was all intended to be the lovely backdrop for abundant life.

Still, Love went on reaching. It was God's reaching that caused Him to put a special value on the human person, that caused God to make man only a little lower than the angels, that gave man the treasure of being able to think and reason, to question and learn—to laugh and cry, to weep and rejoice.

But man misused this gift, distorted and wasted his thinking, perverted his emotions, violated his sensitivities to the feelings of others, and even used his mind to formulate theories arguing that he himself was the god of the universe and that his own mind had invented all things.

Still, Love went on reaching. It was God's reaching in love that built safeguards into the universe so this man wouldn't destroy himself. They were simple, timeless guidelines for freedom and joy. But man called them bondage, fetters, chains. He simply didn't understand that the law was Love's safe harbor to protect him from the storms of himself.

Right from the beginning, God's love has reached, and from the beginning, man has refused to understand. But Love went on reaching, risking rejection, offering itself.

Love offered the eternal; we wanted the immediate. Love offered deep joy; we wanted thrills. Love offered freedom; we wanted license. Love offered communion with God Himself; we wanted worship at the shrine of our minds. Love offered peace; we wanted approval for our wars.

Even yet, Love went on reaching . . . *and the Word of the Father became Mary's little Son, and His love reached all the way to where I was.*

It's Still the Greatest Story Ever Told

A woman and an angel, a promise and a song,
A word too grand for any mind to hold,
A tax law and a journey, a stable and some straw —
These tell the greatest story ever told.

O sing, "Glory in the highest — He is come, our Great Messiah!"
Come bow before this awesome mystery.
Mighty God and fragile baby — here a lowly manger holds,
And it's still the greatest story ever told.

A hillside and some shepherds, a blaze of blinding light,
Angels singing carols in the cold;
Eternal revelation to men as dull as stone —
The glorious, greatest story ever told.

O sing, "Glory in the highest — He is come, our Great Messiah!"
Come bow before this awesome mystery.

Mighty God and fragile baby — here a lowly manger holds,
And it's still the greatest story ever told.

Lyric: Gloria Gaither

Music: William J. Gaither and J. D. Miller

❧❧❧ *It's Still the Greatest Story Ever Told*

Everybody loves a good story, and, as Shakespeare said, as long as there are peo-ple, there will always be a story to write about. Thankfully, as long as there are people who love a good story, writers and storytellers will always be in demand.

Each of us is a story. For some of us, the soap operas on television couldn't hold a candle to the sagas we've lived ourselves. Maybe the reason some of us become addicted to the "soaps" is that they give us a recess from our own stories by intrigu-ing us with someone else's. I've kind of always felt that with so many problems of my own to solve, I didn't need to take on the entanglements of some TV characters.

The success of movies and novels rises or falls on the writer's ability to make a story come alive, to make us identify with one or more of its characters. A skilled writer knows that human nature never changes, and although the details change and the time frames may differ, my story and your story are not so different from the sto-ries of people at any other time and place.

25

Virtues and vices, fidelity and betrayal, innocence and its loss are dramatic forces in the story of mankind, and though the scenario I've lived and the chain of events that shaped you may differ widely, the elements of success or failure, achievement or destruction still are hauntingly similar—be it Cleopatra, Ruth of the Bible, or Hillary Clinton. The character's greatness or fatal flaws aren't that different whether the story is about Hamlet, Julius Caesar, the president of Enron, or the pastor of an American megachurch. The temptation to be seduced by power and control has plagued us since the Garden of Eden and will no doubt be a strong force in this earth's final scene.

It is human nature, too, to think the story is about us. Even in seeking divine guidance for a future we can't see, we human beings tend to ask God for the best writing of our story. We pray, if we're people of prayer, for God to help us with an upcoming career change, or to work out a business deal in our favor, or to cause someone we admire to fall in love with us. We ask that our bodies be healed, our problems be solved, our bills be paid, or our fortunes be turned. We ask God to show us His will for our lives or, more often, to use His power to cause circumstances to change so that what we hope is God's will actually happens.

The truth is, however, that if we're settling for even a *perfect* playing-out of our life's story, we're settling for too little. Even a great human story is short-lived and soon forgotten. The best accomplishments are soon eclipsed by those of another player, and the most startling of scientific discoveries is soon obsolete. For every achievement of excellence, there is a more excellent record-breaker yet to be born. As the good prophet Isaiah says, "All men are like grass, and all their glory is like the flowers of the field . . . The grass withers and the flowers fall, but the Word of our God stands forever" (Isaiah 40:6, 8 NIV).

The good news is that there is a bigger story, a better play, an ultimate drama, and each of us has been cast in a leading role. We have been born to play a part in an eternal story that will never become obsolete. No one can play our part better. No one else can play our part at all.

It is God's story, a story of cosmic proportions with cosmic consequence. Its time frame is all-time and beyond-time. Its setting is here and now and will always be—both historic and present tense. Our character was written into the plot by the Author of all things and was in His imagination before the beginning of time.

Consider this: "Long before he laid down earth's foundations, he had us in mind, had settled on us as the focus of his love, to be made whole and holy by his love" (Ephesians 1:4 THE MESSAGE). We've always been part of the script. We didn't have to audition, show our credentials, or turn in an Oscar-winning performance. Neither did we choose the script. It was written with us in mind.

The play is about God, and in it we have a role of distinction: We play one of His own children. The only part more major—in fact, it is the *reason* we were written into the play at all—is the role of the eldest Son. The story called for Him to be born, to live, and to die, to buy us a part in the family. Because of His choosing to play that part, the story can be told as it was originally conceived by the Author. It's the story of a loving Father, a Son who died to buy back the other siblings who had been sold into slavery, and the playing-out of their growing relationship with the Father, the elder brother, and the rest of the family.

There have been other stories, and there will be stories to come, but there is only one Story. That's why we love it so and never tire of hearing it. We know the characters. We *are* the characters. We recognize the plot—the protagonist, the antagonist, the victims, and the victimized. And we know in the end, the very end, there will be reconciliation of those who have been estranged.

It is still the greatest story ever told. It is the *only* story ever told.

It's Not an Easy Thing to Bear the Son of God

❧❧❧❧❧❧❧❧❧❧❧❧❧❧❧❧❧❧❧❧❧❧❧❧❧❧❧❧❧❧❧❧

There's a dusky silhouette
Etched against an evening sky,
Weary travelers, tired and spent;
Destination now in sight.
Woman tries to bear the pain,
For her time is very near,
While her husband asks again
If they may find lodging here.
But once more there is no room;
They must find another place.
There's a baby coming soon;
Mothers need a quiet space.
O she'll deliver earth a King
Made of spirit and the sod,
But it's not an easy thing
To bear the Son of God.

Three foreboding silhouettes
Etched against a blackened sky,
Once again to pay a debt
The stranger now has to die—
And once again the weight of pain
Makes a figure slump below,
Mother weeping in the rain
For the Son that she loves so.
All the heavens heave a sigh
And earth shudders, "It is done."
Caverns amplify the cry:
"It is finished; it is won!"
Soldiers take the body down
And the mother bears the weight,
But to bear the Son of God
Oh, it's not an easy thing.

A bright, new dawn,
Women running from a tomb—
The body—it is gone!
Like a baby from the womb.
All the earth begins to sing
And the mother knows it's true
It's not an easy thing
But the Son has born her, too.

❦❦❦ *It's Not an Easy Thing to Bear the Son of God* and *Mary's Song*

Our first baby was born very close to Christmas; there are many reasons I'm thankful for that, not the least of which is that it made me, more closely than I might otherwise, identify with what the mother of Jesus was experiencing the days and weeks surrounding the birth of her baby. I tried to imagine, for instance, what it must have been like to travel on the back of a donkey over primitive roads to Bethlehem. No wonder the poor girl went into labor!

And, because we travel so much and have more than once arrived in a strange city only to find that for some reason the hotel had no record of our reservation, I had an inkling of how panic must have risen in Mary's throat when she saw Joseph coming toward her, shaking his head, just as another contraction started.

It probably didn't help that by the time they arrived, it was night. Doesn't night always make every problem seem more insurmountable? Was she chilled—both from the drop in her blood pressure and from the chill of the desert after the sun went down?

It seems to me we tend to glamorize and glorify this all-too-human happening. The lack of privacy was no doubt humiliating. Labor pains hurt worse and tend to go on longer when you're delivering a first child. Husbands may be tender and caring, but when a girl is about to have a baby, she wants her mother around, and a midwife, too, with whom she feels secure in their knowing what to do if there is a problem. Mary was a real girl having her first very real baby.

I was poignantly aware of all these considerations as I went through the birth of my baby. I wondered what Mary felt about "welcoming" a bunch of scruffy shepherds—or any guests, for that matter—right after she'd given birth in the corner of a stable on a pile of straw. Was she weak from loss of blood? Did she nearly pass out trying to stay awake and alert for them? Did she worry about filth around her new baby? Did one of the shepherds ask to hold Him? Was the baby crying? Did she worry about comforting Him or getting Him to start nursing? Was Joseph sensitive and protective? Did he know what she was thinking?

Afterward, when the shepherds went away and told everyone they met in this overcrowded town that the Messiah had been born and they had seen Him with their own eyes, did the guests keep showing up? When did Mary rest? When did Joseph move her? Did the innkeepers finally find a room and move them inside, or did Mary get on that donkey again and ride back to Nazareth carrying a baby in her arms?

I'm fairly sure that at some point, when she finally was alone with her baby, she must have felt a bit possessive of Him. She must have sung to Him in the quiet moments of the night and, though the events she had experienced made her know He wouldn't be hers to hold for long, at least for now He was her baby. How precious these times must have been!

Holding our baby, there were times when I, too, knew she was not really ours, but a loan to us from God for a little time. But, oh, how I treasured that time! I could almost feel the moments ticking away, and I wanted so to make them last. There were moments I'd look at her and wish I could freeze-frame her—halt her progress long enough to keep her for a while. But, I knew that wasn't possible—and so did Mary.

Did she have any idea the huge significance of what was happening to her? Oh, I know she had actually seen an angel, and of all people on earth, she knew without a doubt the circumstances of her child's conception. But did she know that God had chosen to come "close" to us, by trusting His Son into her care? Did she realize then the Word that was in the beginning was wrapped in a baby blanket in her arms?

Did she know that first night that people—broken people, afraid people, estranged and disenfranchised people, poor people, privileged people—could and would come close to a baby and not be afraid? Did she notice as her baby became a toddler and a schoolchild and a preteen, that other children were growing up beside Him, befriended by Him, relaxed around Him?

It must have puzzled her on some days how to reconcile what people had thought for centuries about the way this Messiah would come, and what He'd do once He got here, with this real young man growing up in her house. Did she ever think her son was too meek, too tender, too compassionate, too attentive to "unimportant" people and situations to ever be a great leader?

How often did she re-sing the song that had exploded from her mouth the day

Aunt Elizabeth confirmed the promise within her? Did "My soul doth magnify the Lord, and my spirit hath rejoiced in God my Savior" (Luke 1:46 KJV) still ring in her heart when she saw Him beaten and bleeding under the weight of the cross?

When they took Him down that Friday night and she felt His broken body heavy in her arms, did she think of how this all began with His prenatal body heavy in her swollen womb? Did she look at the three crosses looming above her, silhouetted against the purple sky, and think about the night the three figures—she, Joseph, and the donkey—had made their way across the rise into Bethlehem as the sun was setting purple on the horizon?

And that Easter morning when the women found the tomb empty, the grave clothes neatly folded (in the exact manner their people were accustomed to folding a napkin to say, "I will be back"), and an angel telling them He had risen, did their hearts explode in a Magnificat reprise: "From now on all generations will call me blessed, for the Mighty One has done great things for me" (Luke 1:48–49 NIV)?

The weight, at last, was lifted! Did Mary know that after all the bearing of the weight of her son and His mission, He was, in the final analysis, bearing her and her "descendants forever" (Luke 1:55 NIV).

Amen. Alleluia!

Mary's Song

My soul doth magnify the Lord!
My soul doth magnify the Lord!
And my spirit hath rejoiced,
Rejoiced in God,
In God, my Savior.

For He hath regarded
My humble estate,
Now all generations
Shall call me blessed.

The Mighty hath done great things,
Holy is His name.
He hath filled all the hungry;
Holy is His name—forever:

My soul doth magnify the Lord!

Lyric: Luke 1:46–50. Adapted by Gloria Gaither
Music: William J. Gaither and Bill George
Copyright © 1983 by Gaither Music Company and Yellow House Music.

Listen to the Angels Singing

Listen to the angels singing—
Listen to the angels singing—
Singing, "Gloria! Gloria!"
Listen to the angels singing—
Listen to the angels singing—
Singing, "Gloria! Gloria!"
Who ever thought
That a baby would have brought
    the good news?
Hear the angels singing!

Loping out across the desert,
Trudging through the shifting sand,
Peering at the constellations, hasten
    Scholars from a distant land,
        Across the sand
                Across the land

Where a new star is shinin' tonight
And, don't you know that it's right overhead and in sight
of where the angels are singing.

Something's stirring on the hillside—
Sheep are restless in the fold—
Young man stirring dying embers, remembers
Stories told him by the old
In the cold—
Stories old.
Then the sky starts exploding with light
And then the night is a circus of bright shiny wings—
Glory—Angels singing!

38

Lyric: William J. Gaither and Gloria Gaither
Music: William J. Gaither, Michael Sykes, and Woody Wright
Copyright © 2001 by Gaither Music Company, Mal 'N A1 Music, and Would He Write Songs.

❧ *Listen to the Angels Singing* and *Shepherd's Song*

*I*f the angels sang their announcement of the Messiah's birth, what was the tune? What was the rhythm? We know it was joyous, and it got the shepherds' attention—it must have been some kind of music that spoke to average shepherds. They weren't classical music buffs, after all, and there was no time for a quick refresher course in music appreciation.

It seems that God has a habit of making His utterances in forms we can understand. When God communed with Adam and Eve, His voice was not only clear and precise (Name the animals, eat all the plants and herbs; don't eat of the Tree of Knowledge of Good and Evil), but welcome (They looked forward to walking with Him in the cool of the day).

When God spoke to Moses, His voice came from a bush that burned but "was not consumed" (Exodus 3:2 KJV). God also spoke to the children of Israel thunderously and in smoke, from a dark cloud, and through an earthquake. He wrote with His finger on a tablet of stone, lest there be any mistaking what He needed His people to know.

Samuel, young and innocent, heard God calling him softly by name in the silence of the night. To David, God spoke not only through an angel, but often through inspiration as he played on his lyre under the night sky.

For Ezekiel, the troubling Spirit of the Lord "came upon" him and told him what to say to the people, but God spoke to Balaam through his donkey because Balaam was too insensitive to recognize an angel in his path when he saw one.

So, how did God "sing" His message to shepherds? Could it be to the rhythmic bleating of the flock the shepherds were tending that the angels started to sing, the volume swelling until the shepherds finally realized it was more than sheep they were hearing? Music! It was music! And the light that started out as a bright moon and unusually evident stars—how bright did it have to get before the shepherds looked up to see the heavens alive with angels?

How like God to sing His song to the least likely! Not the faculty at the conservatory; they would have critiqued it. Not the players of the royal symphony; they might have insisted on another key. No. God made His announcement to shepherds, and, at first, the song probably sounded a lot like the sweet night lowing of sheep with lambs.

And to what drumbeat did the Magi ride for miles across the desert? Was there a tune that kept going through their heads as their camels plodded across the soft sand? Could they have sung the ancient word that meant "bright promise," the *wonder* has returned? "Gloria! Gloria!" I don't know, but I do know it's just like God to speak to us all right where we are, in the rhythms of our regular lives, so we might come to recognize the singing of angels and the very whisper of God.

Shepherd's Song

Music? Do I hear music?
Could there be music, or am I getting old?
Yet . . . I thought I heard a song.
Singing? Did I hear singing?
Could there be singing?
The night is so dark and cold,
How could there be a song?

Music! Yes! I heard music!
There can be music . . . I'm not just hearing things!
I'm the one who heard the song!
And I hear singing! Yes! There is singing!
Music and singing . . .
Into this world so cold . . .
There is born to us . . .
A Song!

To the town, the town of Bethlehem!
We must go and worship Him!
Angels . . . did I see angels?
Could there be angels?
Am I just seeing things?
Yet, I know, I know I heard a song!

41

Lyric: Gloria Gaither
Music: William J. Gaither
Copyright © 1983 by Gaither Music Company (ASCAP).
International copyright secured.
All rights reserved.

It's a Time for Joy

It started with an angel—
It started with a star—
It started with a stable—
Astrologers who'd traveled far.
It started with some shepherds
Amazed to find the story true—
A baby in a manger bed
Was God right here for me and you.

The candles in the window—
The carols in the snow—
The gifts that say, "I love you"—
The starlight's gentle glow—
The fire that warms my spirit—
Our laughing baby boy—
I want to thank You, Jesus—
For everything that brings me joy.

It's a time for singing—
It's a time for friends—
It's a time for wrapping packages to send—
It's a time for hugging
Everyone you meet—
It's a time for baking all their favorite treats—
It's a time for secrets
No one knows but you—
It's a time for family and neighbors, too.
It's a time for children—
A time for toys
But mostly it's a time for joy!

Lyric: Gloria Gaither
Music: William J. Gaither, Michael Sykes, and Woody Wright
Copyright © 2001 by Gaither Music Company, Mal 'N Al Music, and Would He Write Songs.

It's a Time for Joy

Christmas is a time for giving, for bringing provisions and resources that not only will delight a loved one, but will be useful in some unexpected way in the future. It is a time for lavish exceptions to practical rules.

We often give clothes a child will grow into, toys children have only dreamed of having, or some treasure that may be even more meaningful as the child matures—like a precious heirloom or a piece of poetry or art created by a grandparent the young person never knew.

Little did Mary and Joseph know when the wise men brought gold, frankincense, and myrrh how those seemingly impractical gifts would one day serve them. Perhaps these stargazers were even wiser than we think, seeing a coming need for travel money, perfume to use as barter, and embalming spices for a premature interment.

At our house, there is an old Irish custom that came to me from my grandmother on the Sickal side and, I suppose, from all the Mahoneys before her. We race to be the first to yell "Christmas gift!" when we visit one another's houses on Christmas morning. With the advent of technology, this has turned into a telephone happening for our family. At each of our houses, the phone will ring early Christmas morning. We know by now to waste no time saying "Hello." We grab the phone and shout "Christmas gift!" The one answering the call almost always wins, since the caller can't predict exactly which ring will bring the response.

My kids call the cousins—my sister's grown girls—who all are, as of now, living in Kansas with their own families. "Christmas gift!" we yell across the miles, pulling them and their little ones in close to hearth and home with our ancient greeting.

Jesus; it's Jesus, the greeting reminds us. *He is the Gift. He is Christmas. Let's start this day remembering the Gift that truly goes on giving.*

Then come the coffee, the juice, and the Story. The other gifts can't be opened until the Story of the real Christmas Gift is read from Luke 2. No makeup, no showers or hairdos, still in pajamas, we are shockingly, disarmingly real to one another as the familiar words are read. If we wanted to, we all could say the words from memory. (I learned and delivered them in church when I was four.) But we all listen, instead, while the Christmas tree laden with familiar ornaments and lights reminds us of the truth behind the symbols.

> And there were in the same country shepherds abiding in the field, keeping watch over their flock by night. And, lo, the angel of the Lord came upon them, and the glory of the Lord shone round about them: and they were sore afraid. (Luke 2:8–9 KJV)

Somewhere out of the blur of activities and the exhaustion of preparations, out of the anticipation of gathering this day yet to come, here in this much-worn living room lined with our motley assortment of pajama-clad human beings, the truth dawns of God's insistent, persistent reach toward us. The Gift—the lavish unlimited provision of grace, given before we even knew we needed it—this great Gift descends upon us all like dew on thirsty plants. We drink it in. We turn our faces toward the words.

The children and their parents look to see if I am crying. I am. I can't help it. In grateful celebration of this Gift, we have cleaned and cooked and kept secrets and hoarded resources and sacrificed to make and find things to delight one another. We have secretly written poems and painted pictures and sewn garments and baked cookies for those we love because He has taught us to "love one another; as I have loved you" (John 13:34 KJV). Simple exhaustion, aching backs, sore feet—these are nothing . . . for love.

I see the gifts under the tree—the beautiful ones, the simple ones, the ones with crooked bows on hand-stamped butcher paper. They are only symbols, really. What would I give the children that would outlast all the secrets bought and made with such careful intentions? What would endure beyond the silk scarves, leather jackets, and pleated wool skirts? What would still serve them after they've outgrown the boots and the sleds and the skates? What would be even more valuable after the gold and silver rings have tarnished, the instruments have been laid aside, and arthritis has caused them to put down their tennis rackets and golf clubs?

Christmas gift! I hear it still echoing through my mind. "And she brought forth her firstborn son, and wrapped him in swaddling clothes" (Luke 2:7 KJV). What would I give the children . . . because of Him?

It's Christmas

Silver bells jingle and lights start to twinkle.
It's Christmas!
Snowflakes are falling and friends come a-calling.
It's Christmas!
Carolers singing and church bells are ringing
They're wishing us all hope and cheer.
The reds and the greens paint a holiday scene
And it tells us that Christmas is here!

Store windows sparkle, the trees in the park say,
"It's Christmas!"
Folks stop to smile and they visit awhile, yes,
It's Christmas!
Shoppers are jostling and neighbors are wassailing
Horses are pulling a sleigh,
That's packed full of kids, full of secrets forbidden
To share 'til they wake Christmas day.

There's no happier season full of peace and good cheer;
And there's a very good reason—
God came to live with us here, with us here!

When a manger and stable are out on the table
It's Christmas!
Shepherds and wise men, a star in the sky says,
"It's Christmas!"
Joseph and Mary and children who carry
A lamb they will give to the Babe,
Wrapped up in swaddling clothes—as everybody knows—
This means it's Christmas day!

God wrapped in baby clothes
Let everybody know
This means it's Christmas day!
It's Christmas!

Lyric: Gloria Gaither
Music: Geron Davis
Copyright © 1995 by Gaither Music Company and DaviSongShop.

❧❧❧ *It's Christmas*

Celebrations rise up around a discovery of something intensely true. When a reality—birth, death, spiritual conversion, a passage of life, falling in love, marriage—uniquely intersects with our own experience, human beings want to mark this moment. We need a way to vent our joy and to create a remembrance for later—later when the aura fades or the going gets tougher. We need to make a place to point back to, a sort of ground zero or point of true north to which we can realign our priorities and reaffirm our commitments.

Celebrations are always a result. Something changes us. We celebrate. A transition, a new direction, a long-awaited breakthrough—these are cause for a party.

Celebrations also tend to become milestones. They are metaphors for progress. They remind us that we're more than machines and that life is more than trudging through the trenches of routine. Somewhere, deep inside, that eternal part of us knows that there is more. That "something else" is what confirms us, insists that we matter, have some lasting consequence. When life events confirm this in some tangible way, we celebrate, and celebrations repeated to help us remember those moments of "breaking through" become sacred rituals.

The birth of a baby, for example, gives us tangible evidence that we, too, were once perfect, innocent, unspoiled. For the moment, we stand in awe of this new life, of God's persistent belief in our capacity to change, to be transformed. It makes us stop blaming the people and things that damaged us and causes us to see that we have a chance to "do it differently." Can we break the old patterns? Can we find the virtues to shape this child without wounding?

Someone dies. Immediately we are reminded of our own mortality, and something stirs inside us that says we must take account of ourselves while we still can. We, too, will die. The mortality rate, last time I checked, was 100 percent. Celebrations of a life that is finished are called for, and at the same time, an assessment of how all we living are spending our days and energies.

Anniversaries of births, commemorations of deaths, weddings to solemnize and to celebrate the union of two lives and histories, and passages—coming of age, retirement from vocation, or leaving for college, military service, or a new venture—all these call for celebrations to mark the moments and make them meaningful.

Cakes, candles, gifts, flowers, songs, games, pictures—these are ways we ritualize the things that can't be adequately expressed in mere words: love, sadness, relief, pride, gratitude, hope, loss, joy, fear. Symbols and metaphors shared by a family or a community intensify our awareness of the importance of moments like these. When we can't really say those things that matter most, we turn to nature or to the artists or the poets to help us. We create traditions—the doing of a thing the same way to make it uniquely "ours." Over time, these rituals and celebrations become a shared history and give us rich soil from which to grow our families into the future. We remind one another with these meaningful moments that we are more than animals, inspire one another to reach beyond our baser natures to something holy and fine.

Jane Howard in her book *Families* (Simon & Schuster, 1978) puts it this way: "Real rituals are discovered in retrospect. They emerge around constructive moments, moments that only happen once, around whose memory meanings cluster. You don't choose moments, they choose themselves . . . Good families prize their rituals. Nothing welds a family more than this."

Then in the history of mankind there comes a moment that changes everything for everybody. This event is not just for one family, but for all families, not just for one culture, but for all cultures. It is a birth. But unlike other births, even the births of great people, this birth was foreseen by prophets hundreds of years before, and it was played out exactly as they predicted, every detail. Yet its details were subtle, ordinary in some ways, extraordinary in others.

This event, and the short life of thirty-three years that followed, split history in two so that for ever after, time would be marked as "before" this Man's life and "after." Yet His coming into the world was accessible to even the poorest of the poor; His life was marked by giving value and worth to all He met—men, women, children, the aged, the wealthy, and the destitute.

The message of emancipation He came to spread resonates with joy and relief in the souls of all who embrace it to this day. Lives are changed. My life has been changed.

Over the centuries, people everywhere have celebrated this moment because it brought heaven and earth together. The mystery of how God would choose to clear up the mystery of Himself by coming Himself as a baby is still the most paradoxical of all. It is both intensely *rational*—satisfying all the requirements of both the old Hebrew law of man and the law of God—and bewilderingly irrational and not to be overtaken by human reason.

Our celebrations of this amazing encounter with pure truth need symbols. This truth—God with us—is too great for things like mere cake and ice cream. We have taken our symbols from the event itself: stars, angels, a stable, shepherds, sheep, kings in lavish attire, a treasure chest of gold.

To these we have added ancient symbols that have taken on new and ultimate meanings: *evergreen trees* symbolize new and ongoing life; *bells,* which were used in ancient towers to announce to all within earshot that something important had happened, are a calling together of all to worship; all kinds of bright and beautiful *lights* draw our eyes from darkness to the "Light of the World"; *gifts* extravagantly chosen and wrapped remind us of not only the gifts brought by the Magi but of the ultimate gift of this Messiah's life in substitution for us all.

Let's tell the children this story. It is not only a true story, it is the story of pure Truth intersecting our lives. Light the candles! Put lights on the green, green tree! Hang the stars, get out the manger and the stable, the sheep, camels, shepherds, and "wise men from afar." Sing the carols, ring the bells, bake the sweets of celebration.

This Life is not just the hope of a new baby born; this is the Hope of the Ages. This is not just a story to help us aspire to greatness; this is the greatest story ever told and the Story and the Teller still live to empower *us* to greatness. This is not just a passage of life we celebrate, but Life itself.

Ordinary Baby

He was just an ordinary baby; that's the way He planned it, maybe;
Anything but common would have kept Him apart
From the children that He came to rescue,
Limited to some elite few,
When He was the only child who asked to be born,
And He came to us with eyes wide open,
Knowing we're hurt and broken,
Choosing to partake of all our joy and pain.

He was just an ordinary baby;
That's the way He planned it, maybe,
So that we would come to Him
And not be afraid.

He was ordinary with exception of miraculous conception—
Both His birth and death He planned from the start;
But between His entrance and exit was a life that has affected

Everyone who's walked the earth to this very day.
With no airs of condescension
He became God's pure extension,
Giving you and me the chance to be remade.

He was just an ordinary baby;
That's the way He planned it, maybe,
So that we would come to Him
And not be afraid.

Lyric: Gloria Gaither
Music: Dony McGuire

❦ Ordinary Baby
(Written for children and for us all)

In the beginning, God and people were best friends. They were glad to see one another whenever they got together, and when they went for walks in the beautiful garden God had made, they laughed and told each other secrets. They shared everything, and no one was embarrassed or shy.

One day, a stranger showed up in the garden—a jealous and selfish creature—and he disguised himself as a beautiful, colorful serpent. He coaxed the two people to break their promises to God and to ruin the wonderful friendship between the people and God.

Afterward, whenever God came to enjoy His friends, the people were ashamed and acted guilty and afraid. It was as if God and His friends had become strangers and had no one to introduce them to one another again. God knew everything had changed between them and could never be fixed unless a miracle happened.

From then on, God tried to get messages to His friends about how sad He was to lose them and how very much He loved them. He wrote "I miss you" on the sunset. (That had been the time they took walks.) He pulled at people with gentle breezes that felt like the way the wind blew when they ran together down the garden paths. He hoped the people would remember how close they had been to Him.

Over the years, more and more people were born. The mothers and fathers, grandmothers and grandfathers passed on stories to the children about how God had been best friends with the first man and woman long ago—how they talked and sang and laughed together. The stories seemed almost too good to be true. God was so great, so powerful . . . and so far away. But some of the people who told stories were special listeners. They said they could hear God trying to talk to people. They said He wanted His friends back and that one day He would find a way to fix the friendship the lying snake had destroyed.

The people guessed at how God might do this. Some thought if they could be good enough, God might be friends with them again. They tried so hard to be perfect and to keep all the rules they thought would make God happy. But being perfect was way too hard. The people always went to bed at night disappointed in themselves and sad because they knew this was no way to get to know God again.

The listeners said God would send someone to introduce people to Him again, so that God's people could gather with Him in a place they called "God's kingdom."

The people talked about what kind of person God would send. The special listeners said God would send a descendant (a child or grandchild or great-grandchild) of a king. That would make Him a King, too. What kind of King would God send?

Certainly, they thought, He'd be a more awesome king than Saul or Solomon or even good King David. He'd be more powerful than the leader of an army. He'd be more rich and fine than the family who lived in the best house in town.

For centuries people waited . . . and wondered. They came up with all kinds of ideas. Some got so tired of waiting they decided the whole story about God was just something someone made up. But it wasn't!

One night in a tiny, tiny town, God kept His promise. And He didn't send someone to introduce people to God—He came Himself! And He didn't come as a king riding on a white horse or as a rich man dressed in fancy clothes. He didn't come as a president or a governor. He didn't even come as a grown-up!

No, God had planned all along to come in a way we could understand. He chose to come as a baby, because no one would be afraid of a baby! He knew children might be shy if He came as a grown-up, but no one can be shy around a baby.

Now children could grow up, not in His shadow, but beside Him. Like the first people in the garden, children and God would know each other . . . and not be afraid!

So, it was true. God came Himself! He was just an ordinary baby born in a simple barn to a loving mother named Mary and a strong man named Joseph, who made things out of wood. Instead of important-looking doctors to help this baby be born, there was just Joseph. Instead of a story in the newspaper, a real star in the sky stopped over the barn and twinkled in the clear, dark night.

Who would have ever guessed! God thought of the best way to gain back His friends. He would be an ordinary baby. That's the way He planned it, maybe, so that we would come to Him and not be afraid.

❦❧❦ *For as Long as There Have Been Babies . . .*

For as long as there have been babies, there have been rocking chairs and lulla-bies. So often I have rocked our little ones and hummed some tune to still their busy bodies and soothe little nerves. At quiet times like these when the deepest form of communion is taking place between a mother and her baby, hopes and fears, joy and pain find expression in the song that could never be expressed in mere words.

There are conflicts in a mother's heart between the now she holds and the anticipated tomorrow beyond her grasp—the dreams for a child's future and the precious security of the present fleeting moments.

Because she was not able to share the secrets of her heart, Mary, too, must have tucked the longings and questions into understated lullabies as she held in her arms the Savior of the world. For Mary was not only the chosen one, she was a mother. And there were hopes and fears, pride and pain, in those quiet songs in the night.

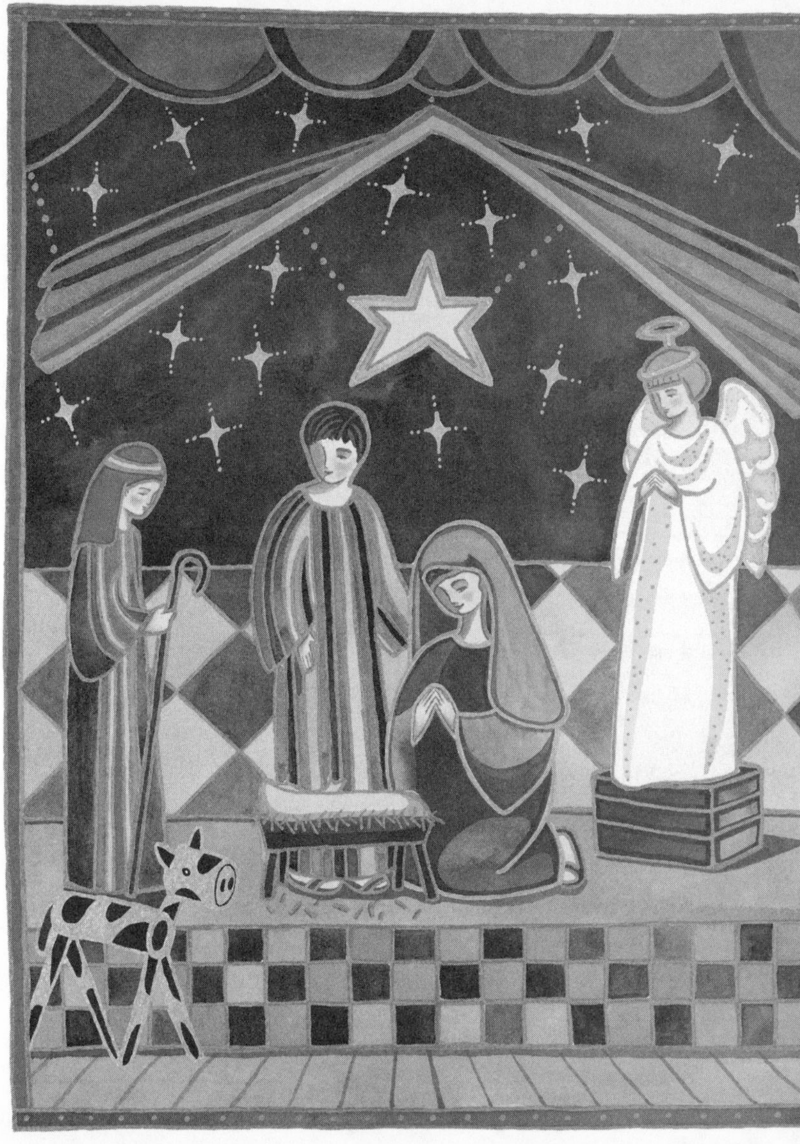

Come and See What's Happenin' in the Barn

~~~
✿❧✿❧✿❧✿❧✿❧✿❧✿❧✿❧✿❧✿❧✿❧✿❧✿❧✿❧✿❧✿❧✿❧✿❧
~~~

Come and see what's happenin' in the barn!
I've seen nothin' like this since I've been on this farm!
Those strangers campin' out there have a baby in their arms—
Come and see what's happenin' in the barn!

Must have been sometime 'bout close to midnight
A big ole guy came knockin' at my door—
He said his wife was 'bout to have a baby,
And she just couldn't travel anymore.
I said the rooms had all been rented out
But they'd find shelter out there in the barn—
They could throw some blankets in the stable;
At least, they would be dry and safe from harm.

Sometime before dawn I was awakened;
Light was floodin' through the windowpane.
A star as bright as moonlight was a-shinin',
And pretty music I could not explain.
I ran downstairs to have a look around,
I tell you I could not believe my eyes—
A crowd had gathered all around the manger
And they were talkin' 'bout God's big surprise.

The shepherds said that they'd been on the hillside
Tellin' stories just to stay awake;
The baby lambs were sleepin' near the campfire,
The ewes were huddled by the stone fence gate.
And then the sky just seemed to open wide—
With light and sound that they could hardly bear,
And what they swore were angels sang in chorus,
"You'll find the new Messiah over there."

Go and see what's happenin' in the barn
There's been nothin' like it ever happened on this farm!
The strangers campin' out there have a baby in their arms—
Go and see what's happenin' in the barn.

Lyric: Gloria Gaither
Music: William J. Gaither, Michael Sykes, and Woody Wright
Copyright © 2000 by Gaither Music Company, Mal 'N Al Music, and Would He Write Songs.

❧❧❧ *Come and See What's Happenin' in the Barn*

When asked, "Where is Alexandria, Indiana?" Bill and I usually reply: "Right in the middle of the cornfields." This is true. Our small town is not only surrounded by fields of corn, soybeans, and wheat, it is in the middle of the state that is surrounded by Illinois, Michigan, and Ohio. Beyond Illinois are Iowa, Nebraska, and Kansas. Together we are known as the "Breadbasket of the World."

Like most Midwestern young people, the kids in Alexandria have parents who grew up on working farms, and even though not many farms are as active as they once were, most country and small-town kids still belong to a great organization called 4-H, where life skills are taught like sewing, canning, baking, woodworking, model-building, and raising farm animals.

The county 4-H fair is held every July in our own Beulah Park, where the work of these young people is judged and the prize livestock is auctioned for top dollar. Restaurants in our area proudly advertise that their gourmet establishments serve the blue-ribbon-winning beef, pork, or poultry.

Alexandria is a good place to live because of solid farm families who would still set an extra place at the table if you happened in at suppertime, pull your car out of a snowdrift in the winter with their tractor, or water and feed your dog while you are on vacation. A few of the country places around small towns like ours have turned the extra space in their big houses into bed-and-breakfast inns since the kids are grown and gone.

So it isn't hard for Bill and me to imagine an innkeeper taking in extra people in a town too small for big hotels, and feeding them, too. It isn't hard to imagine how bad the farmer and his wife must have felt when, in spite of their NO VACANCY sign, a weary man and an about-to-deliver pregnant girl knocked at the door.

"Every bed in the house is full," he must have said before he noticed the grimace on the face of the young woman. "Why, Joe," his wife must have said, "that girl's in labor. We can't let that baby be born in the street."

"Here. Tell you what we'll do," the farmer must have offered. "Come on around to the stable. There's new straw to throw down, and we'll make a place where you'll have some privacy. Maud, here, will bring you some hot water and linens; they're worn, but they're clean. You can tie your donkey under the overhang."

Because of that one little clause in Luke's Gospel—"because there was no room for them in the inn" (2:7 KJV)—these innkeepers have sometimes gotten a bad rap. But knowing farmers as we do, I think these people went out of their way to give this couple the only other shelter they had.

Can you imagine their surprise as the night wore on? Stars stopping over their stable, shepherds making a ruckus about angels singing on the hillside, and then, strangers inquiring about the newborn for weeks afterward.

They'd seen a lot of births in their time. Farmers tend to take such things in stride. But this was no ordinary birthing. These country folk must have had quite a story to share that night and the next few weeks at the Farm Bureau meeting.

All too often, we turn the characters in this real-life drama into celebrities or deities. There was only one Deity there that night. The rest were ordinary people experiencing an extraordinary happening. But at the time, they all did the best they could with what they had: some swaddling clothes Mary had no doubt brought with her, a feeding trough turned baby cradle, a rough cloak or two, some clean straw, and a stable made warm enough for a newborn by the body heat of some farm animals.

The rest is history . . . and prophecy.

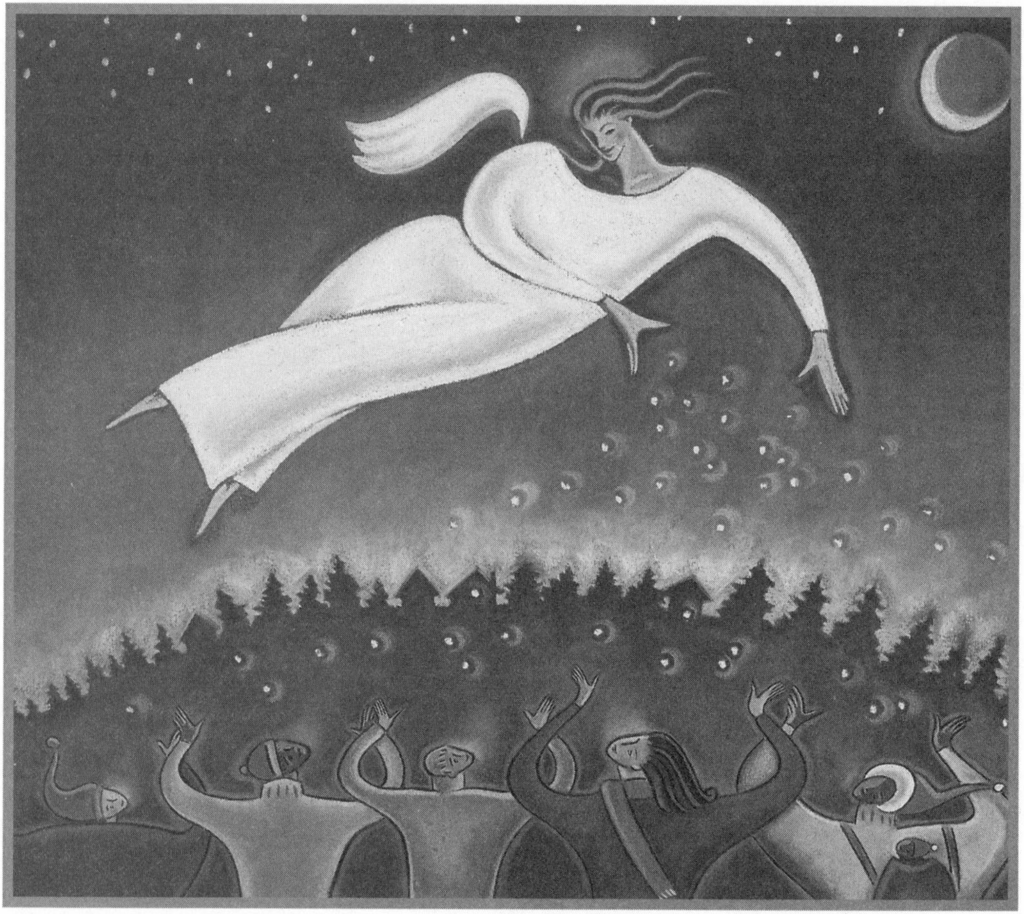

Unspeakable Joy

Joy, joy, unspeakable joy!
Music is filling the air.
Glory, oh, glory to God!
Angels are everywhere.

Promised Messiah!
Our Immanuel!
Alpha, Omega, and King!
The Hope of the Ages
At last has been born!
Let's join all creation and sing!

Come and adore Him—
Young Mary's sweet boy—
There in the manger asleep.
Eden's deep wound
Will be taken away
By the Lamb lying there with the sheep!

67

❦❦❦ *Unspeakable Joy*

Our family's history with the gospel-singing Goodman family goes way back. When our first baby, Suzanne, was only nine or ten months old, she loved the rhythms that this Kentucky family created. Like flicking on a switch, she would start to dance when we put a Goodman recording on the stereo. Because she was just starting to walk, Bill would pick her up and let her sit in the palm of his hand over the back of the couch so her tiny feet could just touch. He would bounce her up and down to the beat of "Oh, I wouldn't take nothin' for my journey now; I gotta make it to heaven somehow…" Her little hands would clap and her eyes would sparkle at the magic this family could create. Soon she had her own version: "I wouldn't take nothin' for my Jersey cow," she would sing at the top of her lungs.

Just a couple of years shy of forty years later, Bill and I were driving to Indianapolis for dinner. We were planning a Christmas videotaping with what had come to be known as the Homecoming Friends. We had decided to call the video *Christmas in the Country,* and we were writing and looking for new Christmas songs with a down-home country flavor. Bill had written some music with that "Goodman feel" the week before and had brought a rough tape of the tune with him that night.

He has a sneaky way of playing a piece of music for me over and over so it will start to bug me that it doesn't have words. He'd been doing this intermittently at home—a sort of subliminal reminder that I had work to do.

This night, trapped in the car going seventy miles an hour, he had my full attention. He also had a "hook" and part of a chorus. "Joy, joy, unspeakable joy la-la-la-la-la-la-la," he sang.

Sure enough, he had me hooked on the music by then. I had a tablet with me "just in case," so I took it out and began to write. I could hear first Howard, then Vestal singing the verses by turn as I wrote down what the music seemed to be saying:

Promised Messiah!
Our Emmanuel!
Alpha, Omega, and King!
The Hope of the Ages
At last has been born!
Let's join all creation and sing!

I handed the tablet to Bill. He held it on the steering wheel and sang the words to the music. "That fits! That's really good," he said, grinning.

He handed back the tablet. "Write another verse."

Now it was Vestal's turn in my head:

Come and adore Him—
Young Mary's sweet boy—
There in the manger asleep.

Eden's deep wound
Will be taken away
By the Lamb lying there with the sheep!

I handed the tablet back to Bill. Little did the cars on Interstate 69 know that a song was coming between them and perfect safety. I like to think God sent an angel to take a turn at the wheel as Bill sang the second verse. When he got to the "Eden's deep wound" part he sort of got stuck.

"Wait—how does this go?" We rewound the tape and I sang it for him.

As usual, I like the part best that he questioned. I still do. I always have a hard time telling just the Christmas story without the rest of the Story. I had to at least tell it in symbol and metaphor.

"I like it!" he said when we got through the second chorus. "Let's call Vestal."

We did call Vestal and read it to her right then and there. Together we rejoiced in a new telling of an old, old story.

After Bill made the sound track in the studio, we tried out the song with Howard and Vestal. It pleased us both that it fit them like a glove, and it pleased them that we had written this new song of joy just for them.

They sang it at the Christmas taping in Birmingham. Little did we know that Howard would be here only one more Christmas season to sing it. But Vestal got on the bus after his death and traveled for another year. With the Hoppers, she sang it each night of the 2003 Christmas season concerts, her verse strong and clear.

Because Howard died before Christmas the year before, she thought it would be sad to have Christmas at home without him. Her family had decided to take her with them to Florida to celebrate Christmas and to rest. Then she was to meet the Homecoming singers in Charlotte for Jubilaté.

But the Hope of the Ages had plans to let her celebrate not just a new year but a new age with her Howard. There is music where they are, and they are singing again together. As a songwriter, I can't help hoping there might be at least one more chorus of . . .

Joy, joy, unspeakable joy!
Music is filling the air.
Glory, oh, glory to God!
Angels are everywhere!
  Angels are everywhere!

Christmas in the Country

Oh, there's nothing like Christmas in the country—
The simple joy of family by the fire
And carols ringing out across the valley
From neighbors that make up the village choir.
Oh, the joy of Christmas in the country
The love and warmth and gentle memories—
And knowing that the simple old sweet story
Is waiting in the country just for me.

The smell of fudge and apples from the kitchen—
The bubble lights that flicker on the tree—
The whispered sounds of secrets from the children
Embrace and call back home the likes of me.

There's nothing like Christmas in the country
When silent snow is falling on the barn,
And children press their noses to the window
As winter turns to magic the old farm.

Oh, the joy of Christmas in the country
The love and warmth and gentle memories—
And knowing that the simple old sweet story
Is waiting in the country just for me.

The laughter stops as Pop picks up the Bible
It falls from habit open to Luke 2
And none of us will ever tire of hearing,
"Now children, here is how God came to you."

"There were in that same country shepherds
watching
The flocks at night upon a lonely hill . . ."
And with his well-worn voice he tells the story
Of how God loved us once and loves us still.

73

Oh, the joy of Christmas in the country
The love and warmth and gentle memories—
And knowing that the simple old sweet story
Is waiting in the country just for me.

Lyric: Gloria Gaither
Music: William J. Gaither, Michael Sykes, and Woody Wright
Copyright © 2000 by Gaither Music Company, Mal 'N Al Music,
and Would He Write Songs. All rights reserved.

❧❧❧ *Christmas in the Country*

I believe there is a homing device in every human heart. Even if we've never had a good home to go home to, there is an innate yearning for one where we are cherished and understood. In our yearning, we see this as a place of peace where there is no pretense and where we are accepted for who we truly are—not for what we've accomplished or how we look.

And there is no time like Christmas for pulling us back to such a place. Usually, how much we love and look forward to Christmas as a holiday is in direct proportion to how close to this ideal home really is. Sadly, for many the reality of the holiday is one of the most painful experiences of the year.

Perhaps the reason we cling to the ideal at Christmas more than at any other time is that this celebration is in honor of the One who came to bring true peace, joy, love, and a place to belong. And the truth is that no family home and no human relationship can ever totally give us what we need. Every parent fails sometimes. Every love falls short. Every child disappoints and turns prodigal at one time or another. No sibling is totally supportive or faithful to protect the secrets with which he or she has been entrusted.

Even so, home is the nearest thing we have to a metaphor for belonging. The imperfection of us all keeps us yearning for another place—the place that will truly be Home.

Thankfully, our memories tend to preserve the good and forgive the flawed. I'm sure my grandma's house in the country was not as good as I remember it. The "front room," as she called it, was not as big, the kitchen not as warm, the snows not as white or as deep as in my memories of trudging through them to get to that farmhouse with the fieldstone porch.

As I recall, she and Grandpa opened the big double doors to that front room only for special occasions. The piano was in there, and she would always have the old itinerant piano tuner come just before Christmas so we could sing carols around that piano when we all crowded in.

The Christmas tree she put in that room was not a pine, but a cedar tree Pa would cut fresh from the woods behind the barn. The ornaments were of World War II vintage and before—scenes painted on clear glass balls—and there were strips of foil we called "ice sickles," big lights of every color, and real candy canes. Grandma would always make fresh popcorn balls with sorghum molasses, wrap them in a new thing called Saran Wrap, and hang them on the tree for us kids to "snitch" when no one was looking.

Grandma baked for days before Christmas: pies of apples and cherries from their orchard, fudge, taffy, divinity layered in boxes between buttered sheets of waxed paper, cinnamon rolls for breakfast, and homemade bread. These were all prepared before the real cooking started.

To this day I find myself running my fingers over mixing bowls in antiques shops that have brown and gold sheaves of wheat on them or picking up green Fire King baking dishes and pie pans, longing to take them home to see if they would somehow turn things I make into the magical tastes of my childhood for my grandkids to remember.

Country life always seemed to separate the boys and the men from the women and the girls. The guys would "mosey" out to the barn to talk to Pa while he milked the two cows they always kept to supply them with milk and butter. The boys would help him throw down hay for the night, feed the cats, and gather the eggs from the henhouse. On summer mornings gathering eggs was Grandma's job, but in the winter when she was less sure of her footing, Pa brought in the eggs.

Meanwhile, the women would take up stations in the kitchen peeling potatoes, opening jars of green beans Grandma had canned the summer before, and cutting up squash, onions, brussels sprouts, and turnips. The girls would set up the table in the living room, then work on the jigsaw puzzle that became a family project all through the days of Christmas.

I don't remember much about the gifts. They were simple, practical, and usually handmade. I do remember hugs and "thank you's." I remember Grandma loving whatever I gave her as if she'd been wanting it all her life. I have a picture of someone in our family holding up a string of pearls—probably ordered from the Sears catalog ("the wish book," we called it)—and looking as if this necklace were as precious and rare as diamonds.

There was never any doubt why we had Christmas. Since Grandma had lost most of her eyesight, my daddy read the Christmas story from Luke while the children sat on someone's lap or on the floor, leaning back on some seated grown-up's knees. We all knew the words by heart, but familiar as they were, they always brought tears to our eyes—as though we were hearing this wonderful story for the first time.

Grandma would pray, and when she prayed the angels quit swishing their wings and got still. We knew that sooner or later every one of our names would be specifically mentioned; Grandma would thank the Lord for the gift of each one of us and ask His tender care and guidance as we grew and changed and became what He intended for us to be.

After prayer and presents, the music would begin. Grandma played both the piano and the guitar; Pa played the "fiddle" and the "mouth harp." We all knew sooner or later he'd grab Grandma by the arm and try to make her dance around the room; she'd say, "Oh, Pop, quit!" And we'd all laugh.

The children would ask for their favorite of the songs that Grandma had always sung to them: "Redwing," "Mockingbird Hill," or "Listen to the Mockingbird." It never seemed strange that all our favorite songs were about birds.

We also sang Grandma's favorites: "What a Friend We Have in Jesus," "I Must Tell Jesus," and "Leaning on the Everlasting Arms."

It seems to me now, looking back, that I was the most adored of children, and I know all the grandchildren would say they thought they were. The truth is, we all were.

As night fell and the kerosene lamps were lit, it seems to me the love in that house could be touched—like soft velvet or the smooth fur of a kitten. The snow could pile to the eaves for all we cared. We were home, we were fed, and we were loved.

When Bill and I started thinking about recording a video for Christmas with the Homecoming Friends that would be *Christmas in the Country,* it was the images of Christmas at Grandma's house that came to mind. To that I added the memories of my own childhood home and the rituals that have now been handed down first to Bill and me, then to our children, and now to their children.

Someday there will be a new celebration in a new Country. There will be no gap between the ideal and the reality; the relationships around that circle will be perfect and totally beautiful. There will be songs of thanksgiving and praise for Christmas completed, for the One who brought heaven to earth will have then brought earth to heaven, and we all will finally be home.

A Prayer for Christmas

Lord, thank You for being so persistent and so very patient with us, even though often we've failed to recognize Your hand reaching in our lives. And even though often we've actually rejected Your direction to follow our own selfish whims, still You forgave us . . . and more, You've even offered us a way to share in Your very own life. Thank You, Lord.

Christmas in Indiana

I'm spendin' Christmas in Indiana
Where the folks never change;
Everyone knows your name.
Can't wait to be back in Indiana,
Where the rivers still freeze
And the snow weights the trees;
I'm gonna catch a flight come Friday night,
So I can hold you close by the candlelight;
And we'll love again
Just like we did back then in Indiana.

I'm spending Christmas in Indiana
In every window there'll be
A flick'ring candle for me.
Can't wait to be back in Indiana;
There'll be a wreath on the door,
And we'll be singing once more

All the carols we knew
Back when I sang with you
In the city square
With all our friends back there;
In the silent night
It will all be right in Indiana.

There's a place on the edge of town
That I can't wait to see
Where the house is warm and I'll find again
The little child in me.
Supper is waiting—the log is ablaze,
And the children are gazing at magical bright lights
That glitter and dance to sweet music.

I'm spendin' Christmas in Indiana
Where the folks never change;
Everyone knows your name.
I'm gonna be back in Indiana
Where the promise is true
That they'll wait for you.

And I will catch a flight come Friday night,
So I can hold you close by the candlelight;
And we'll love again
Just like we did back then in Indiana!

❦❦❦ *Christmas in Indiana* and *Tonight!*

Two of the Christmas songs in this collection were written with my son, Benjamin. Both brought me a lot of joy for different reasons.

The first, "Tonight!," I loved writing because his music was so challenging to me. Born in 1970, Benjy grew up with rock and roll and had a band by the time he was fourteen. The rhythms that pulsated through our house became part of me, too.

He would bring home recordings of his favorite group, and together we would lie on our bellies on the floor of the playroom and listen to his favorite cuts. I usually had the lyric sheets spread out to follow along with such groups as Journey (his favorite), Triumph, and Foreigner.

As he became a grown-up man and a serious songwriter, I watched him branch out stylistically. When he started a company to create animated projects for kids, he began creating the songs and the sound tracks that would speak to the generation following his.

He wrote the music for "Tonight!" as one of his own recording projects. I loved the irregular meter and the way the music seemed to announce the birth of Christ in present tense. I took the cue from his music and wrote the lyric in present tense.

The song was recorded by Benjy's group, then picked up for a choir arrangement by Geron Davis (for Praise Gathering Publications) so that churches could begin their Christmas celebrations with this joyful present-tense arrangement.

The second piece I wrote with Benj was "Christmas in Indiana." I guess this one brought me such joy because I was so pleased to know that our family celebrations in this Midwest prairie setting had been meaningful enough to him that he wanted to celebrate their memory in a song.

When I wrote the lyric I made it very personal; I have learned over my years of writing that to be universal one must be very specific. It is not so much in the wide generalities that we find community with other human beings, but in the small specifics: a cup of coffee, the sounds of cicadas at night, the breath of a baby, the taste of Grandma's peanut brittle.

Whether it is the details of the first Christmas in Bethlehem or the unique quirky way each family celebrates it, God *is* in the details. I am so glad to be one of the details He came here to see to. That's what the Incarnation is all about.

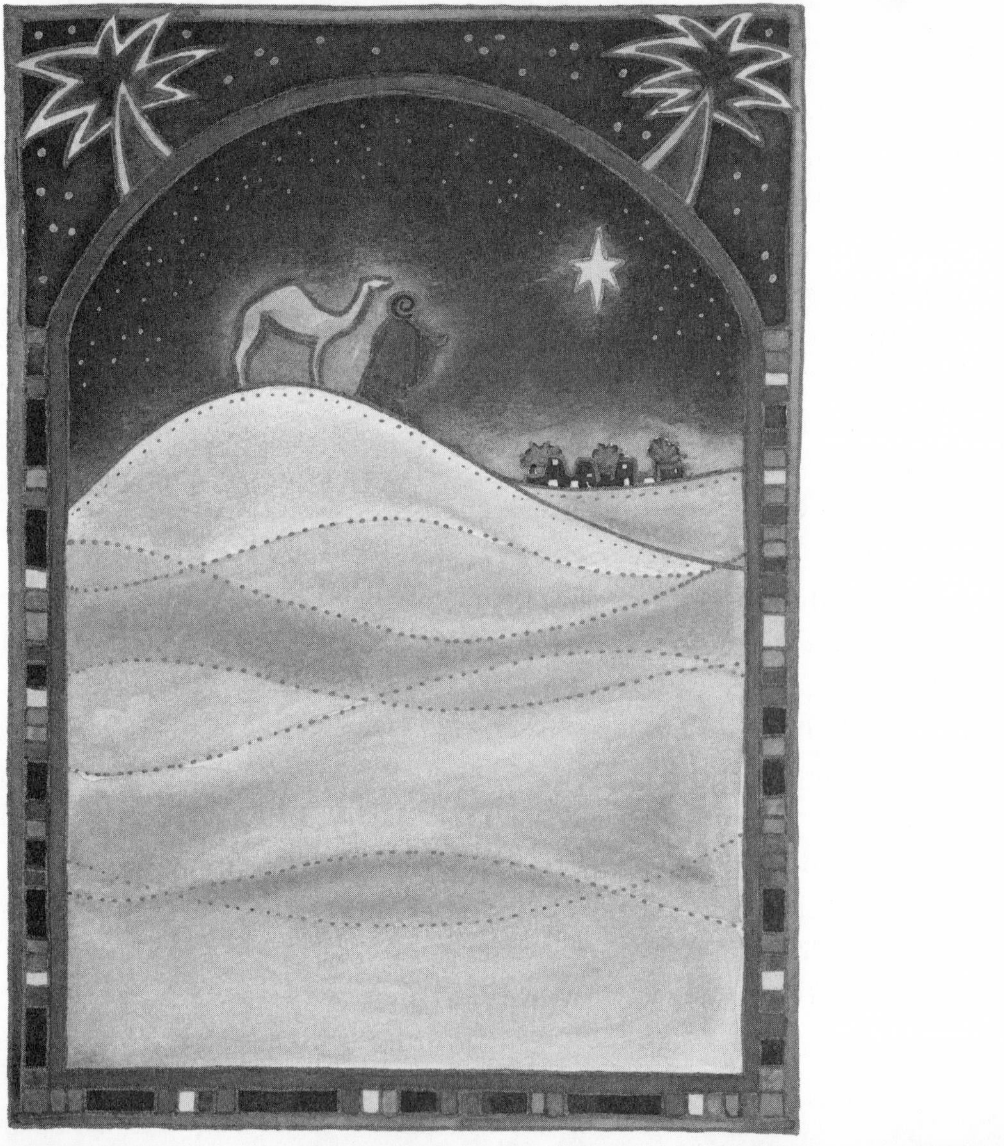

Tonight!

Kings and shepherds make their way
Straight to where a baby lay;
Rich and poor and lonely
Bow before this sight —
A light — a star has led them to this place,
The Word that's been echoing through space
Becomes a child tonight!

Light to shine in the darkest night —
Light to make all the wrong things right —
Light to show everyone the way —
Light to shine where a virgin lay —
Star of David, the prophet's star —
Yahweh — God come to where we are.
Star to make the Messiah's birth,
Star of heav'n now touches earth
Tonight!

Angel voices fill the air —
Angel wings are everywhere —
Light so bright it's blinding —
Shepherds shake with fright.
A song, a warmth begins to flood the hill
"Fear not! Peace to you — goodwill
Comes to earth tonight!"

Light to shine in the darkest night —
Light to make all the wrong things right —
Light to show everyone the way —
Light to shine where a virgin lay —
Star of David, the prophet's star —
Yahweh — God come to where we are.
Star to make the Messiah's birth,
Star of heav'n now touches earth
Tonight!

Light will be so bright
It will shine through the darkest night
Send down Your holy light.

Light to shine in the darkest night —
Light to make all the wrong things right —
Light to show everyone the way —
Light to shine where a virgin lay —
Star of David, the prophet's star —
Yahweh — God come to where we are.
Star to make the Messiah's birth,
Star of heav'n now touches earth
Tonight!

87

Lyric: Gloria Gaither
Music: Benjamin Gaither
Copyright © 1994 by Gaither Music Company, One
on the Line Music, and Ariose Music. All rights reserved.

Three songs in this collection—"Anthem for Christmas," "Old Friends—Christmas," and "Loving God, Loving Each Other"—were adapted for Christmas for the artists who recorded them. The next three pieces are the stories of how this happened.

✿✿✿ *Anthem for Christmas*

"Anthem" is a song I originally wrote with Michael W. Smith, who sent me its beautiful melody and asked if I was interested in writing lyrics for it.

I love writing this way. I listen to music and let the music tell me what the lyric should be. There was such cosmic grandeur and joy in Michael's music that I immediately thought of Psalm 19: *The heavens declare the glory of God,* it begins, *the skies proclaim the work of His hands. Day after day they pour forth speech; night after night they display knowledge* (vv. 1–2 NIV).

How I love this psalm! People have often asked how those who have never heard the story of Christ could ever find God. But this psalm clearly says that the firmament itself is telling the story. The day tells the night and the night tells the next morning about the wonders of God. *There is no speech or language where their voice is not heard* (v. 3 NIV).

How much more direct to the heart of every person can a message be than this? I love the image of the sun as a bridegroom coming out of a wedding tent, dressed to the nines (see vv. 4–5)! No guest at the wedding could miss how strong and handsome he is as he personally goes from guest to guest, welcoming everyone to this great occasion.

Then comes that incredible list of the attributes of God that are published every day by the heavens and all the firmament. If we had only those two things to instruct us about God, this psalm says, we could still deduct these dependable principles:

The Principle	The Quality	The Result
The laws of the Lord	are perfect	revive the soul
The statutes of the Lord	are trustworthy	make the simple wise
The precepts of the Lord	are right	give joy to the heart
The commands of the Lord	are radiant	give light to the eyes (enlightenment)
The fear of the Lord	is pure	endures forever
The ordinances of the Lord	are sure	altogether righteous

The psalmist goes on to say that all of these principles (which the heavens and the firmament declare in each person's own language) are more precious than *much pure gold;* they are *sweeter than honey from the comb* (v. 10 NIV).

How valuable is this? We are both warned and rewarded by these laws, precepts, and ordinances. They are built into the universe and are not victim of human opinion or whim.

They turn us inside out so we can recognize and deal with our own secret sins. But they also heal us when we get it right. Then the psalmist, convicted by the articulate expression of the universe, ends with one of the most beautiful prayers in all of Scripture:

> May the words of my mouth and the meditation of my heart
>> be pleasing in your sight,
>> Oh LORD, my Rock and my Redeemer. (v. 14 NIV)

So, the original song was born of Michael's lovely music and the inspiration of Psalm 19. Later, when Michael W. was making his first Christmas recording, he called and asked if there was any way I could make this anthem into a song for Christmas. The idea of doing that excited me; I knew the coming of the Messiah was the obvious final statement of the Word that had been echoing through the firmament. The Christmas version, then, was recorded as you see it here—with the rest of the story! In italics are the lyrics added for Christmas.

Anthem for Christmas

In the space of the beginning
Was the living Word of Light;
When this Word was clearly spoken,
All that came to be was right.

All creation had a language—
Words to say what must be said;
All day long the heavens whispered,
Signing words in scarlet red.

Amber rays and crimson rainbows,
Twinkling stars and flashing light
Punctuated heaven's statement:
God is glorious, perfect, right.

All creation sings His praises!
Earth and heavens praise His name!
All who live, come join and chorus,
Find the words! His love proclaim!

All day long the sun proclaims it
Like a bridegroom dressed in white,
Coming from his tent to greet them;
All his guests feel his delight.

Words of love and warmth he whispers.
Warming all who hear his voice.
"Oh, be glad and share my table,
Dance and celebrate . . . rejoice!"

Still some failed to understand it.
So God spoke His final Word—
On a silent night in Judah's
Hills a baby's cry was heard.

"Glory!" sang the angel chorus.
"Glory!" echoed back the night.
Love has come to walk among us
God is glorious, perfect—right!

All creation, sing His praises!
Earth and heaven, praise His name!
All who live, come join the chorus,
Find the words! His love proclaim.

Lyric: Gloria Gaither
Music: Michael W. Smith
Copyright © 1988, 1990 by Gaither Music Company and O'Ryan Music, Inc.

Old Friends—Christmas

At the request of Janet Paschal, who wanted a version of the song "Old Friends" for her Christmas recording project, I wrote an extra verse celebrating the gift of friendship at Christmas.

The original song had been Bill's idea and came out of the renewal of friendships through the *Homecoming* videos. I guess the longer we live, the more we come to treasure friendships, especially long-term friendships. We are so blessed to have had so many friends who have—as we girls like to say—been with us "through thick and thin." Literally!

Bill and I wanted the song to be simple enough to seem familiar, like a great old song we've always known, like a good "old friend." I thought that could best be accomplished lyrically by using one of my favorite devices—the series—and in this case, a series of things friends do or send or say to make us know they're there for us.

When we actually sang this song in a roomful of old friends, it seemed natural to pass the phrases around, taking turns with the lines. From then on, it's always been sung that way in concert and on video.

When Janet recorded the Christmas version, she turned the song into a "sitting by the fireplace" kind of ballad, nostalgic and intimate; she has the perfect voice to do that. This, then, is the Christmas version of "Old Friends," and again, the added Christmas lyrics are in italics. I can almost smell the chestnuts roasting!

Old Friends—Christmas

A phone call, a letter, a pat on the back, or a "Hey, I just dropped by to say…"
A hand when we're down, a loan when we just couldn't pay—
A song or a story, a rose from the florist, a note that you happened to send
Out of the blue just to tell us that you're still our friend—

Old friends—after all of these years, just
Old friends—through the laughter and tears
Old friends—what a find! What a priceless treasure!
Old friends—like a rare piece of gold.
Old friends—make it great to grow old.
Old friends—through it all I will hold to old friends.
Oh God must have known
That some days on our own
We would lose our will to go on—
That's why He sent friends like you along.
Old friends—yes, you've always been there,

My old friends—we've had more than our share—
Old friends—I'm a rich millionaire in old friends.

A cold snowy sleigh ride, or carols at midnight, a box someone left by my door,
A bell ringing just to remind me to care for the poor.
Some shepherds and angels, a babe in a manger, a secret that had to be told;
How God made us friends is a story that never grows old.

Oh God must have known
That some days on our own
We would lose the will to go on—
That's why He sent friends like you along.
Old friends—like a rare piece of gold.
Old friends—*brought me in from the cold.*
Old friends—through it all I will hold to old friends.

Lyric: Gloria Gaither
Music: William J. Gaither and J. D. Miller
Copyright © 1993, 1999 by Gaither Music Company, Life Gate Music, and Lojon Music. All rights reserved.

Loving God, Loving Each Other

The Bread of Life, a manger,
A promise and a star,
A girl who loved her God with all her heart;
Sweet music and poor shepherds,
Rich strangers from afar—
Perfect love, a mystery from the start.

An old man and a baby,
A song of thankful praise,
A prophecy of sword-wound to the soul;
The paradox of wonder—
A mother's joy and pain;
A triumph riding bareback on a foal.

Loving God, loving each other,
Making music with my friends;

Loving God, loving each other,
And the story never ends.

They pushed back from the table
To listen to His words,
His secret plan before He had to go;
It's not complicated,
Don't need a lot of rules;
This is all you need to know.

It's loving God, loving each other,
Making music with my friends;
Loving God, loving each other,
And the story never ends.

We tend to make it harder,
Build steeples out of stones,
Fill books with explanations of "the way";
But if we'd stop and listen,
And break a little bread,
We would hear the Master say:

His birth was hardly noticed
His death a public shame,
His life a walk along a dusty road;
His words a revolution,
A fire to melt my chains,
Set me free, and lift my heavy load.

✺✺✺ *Loving God, Loving Each Other*

The Jordanaires were already a household name for gospel music fans when, in the late fifties, there came along a young army sergeant from Tupelo, Mississippi, with a sultry voice and a passion for harmony named Elvis Presley. Almost overnight the Jordanaires found their name in billboard headlines, theater marquees, and the backliners of million-seller recordings.

For years this gospel group backed up Elvis, not only on gospel recordings (the only recordings for which he received Grammy awards) but also on pop and rock-and-roll hits. Their smooth sound was the velvet setting for this new world-famous star.

Other quartets were to follow: The Imperials and the Stamps both had their stint of "backing up Elvis" and "playing Vegas," but the thumbprint of the Jordanaires would remain. Quiet and unassuming, this smooth group was called on time and again to enrich the sound of not only Elvis Presley but other artists such as Patsy Cline, Kenny Rogers, Loretta Lynn, Tennessee Ernie Ford, Tammy Wynette, Dolly Parton, and Ringo Starr, to name a few.

In 2003 this classic group, still in love with gospel harmony, called to see if Bill and I would write for them a Christmas version of one of the songs we had written. They had heard the Vocal Band and the Homecoming group sing it and wanted to include it on what they thought might be their last Christmas collection.

The more I thought about it, the more I realized that what we had originally written was only part of the story; we had left out the first act of the play. The "Loving God, Loving Each Other" story really began when the Word, spoken into the formless void in the very beginning, became "flesh, and dwelt among us" (John 1:14 KJV).

"Yes," we called back to say. "We would be glad to turn 'Loving God, Loving Each Other' into a Christmas song." It should have started with Christmas in the first place.

The details of the Bethlehem birth were not accidental; they were essential in the deepest sense of the term:

~ The town—named the "city of bread," where the Bread of Life would first be cradled in a manger
~ The manger—meaning "to eat," a place to hold grain for the lowly animals to feed
~ The star—reminiscent of the stars God showed to Abraham when He promised to multiply his seed as the stars of the sky
~ The Advent itself—God's touching earth as a seed inside a young and innocent girl, a descendant of Adam and of Abraham
~ The wise men—"those who were afar off," the foreign and wise astrologers included in the very first family of believers

None of this was insignificant, but all part of the amazingly connected story of Love in pursuit of the beloved's heart. My heart. Your heart.

So I began to distill the centuries of details, both prophesied and realized, into two simple verses:

> *The Bread of Life, a manger,*
> *A promise and a star,*

A girl who loved her God with all her heart.
Sweet music and poor shepherds,
Rich strangers from afar—
Perfect love, a mystery from the start.

An old man and a baby,
A song of thankful praise,
A prophecy of sword-wound to the soul;
The paradox of wonder—
A mother's joy and pain;
A triumph riding bareback on a foal.

The stage was set. But the stage was always set for the ending, because the ending was the "why" of His coming. Fast-forward to the last scene—past the healings and the miracles, the beatitudes and the wise words; past the drama of debate and the simplicity of walking the dusty roads—for that, ultimately, was how this great God becoming one of us played out His love story and taught us, the children of His heart, how to live out ours.

Elvis is gone, and so are several others who sang with him. Since Elvis, stars have come and gone; many names have dimmed and flickered out on Vegas marquees. Many of the original recordings can be found in antiques stores and at garage sales.

But the Christmas love story is still best sung, spoken, and lived out by regular people in regular places. And the Jordanaires, bless them, have endeared themselves to us all by going about their regular lives. They have perhaps made their greatest mark of all by living out the really big story of God's love in simple, tender, daily ways. In the end, this is the true measure of us all.

Some Things I Must Tell the Children

How can we tell you the things we must tell you,
The things that we want you to know—
All about living and reasons for giving,
And things that will help you to grow?
Oh, we've watched your diet, taught you to be quiet
In places of worship and school;
We've kept you well groomed with a nice, tidy room,
And we've mentioned the Golden Rule.
But along the way did your heart hear us say
That you don't have to earn our love?
Not a thing you could do could make us stop loving you;
Just the joy that you've brought is enough.
There isn't a thing that the future could bring
That could take back the gift that you are;
You are a treasure we never could measure—
Just some things we must tell the children.

I'm sure we've told you to mind all your manners,
And to get to appointments on time;
And we remind you to hang up your clothes,
And finish the homework assigned.
You've learned to care for your teeth and your hair,
And you make your own bed every day;
You got decent grades and your lunch money's paid,
And you won your first game yesterday.

But did we make it clear; were you able to hear
As you skipped through the house and our lives
That God has a plan that you must understand
No matter how much you "arrive"?
Never stop dreaming, keep working and singing,
But remember just whose child you are.
Stand tall and walk straight, and be home before eight—
Just some things we must tell the children.

And whatever you do, remember: We love you—
Just some things we must tell the children.

Lyric: Gloria Gaither
Music: Bill Gaither
Copyright © 1980 by Gaither Music Company. All rights reserved.

104

❦ *Gifts I Would Give Our Children*

I want to give our children the gift of solitude, the gift of knowing the joy of silence, and the chance to be alone and not feel uncomfortable. I want to give them transportation for the inner journey and water for their desert places. I want to make them restless with shallow diversions and disenchanted with the artificial excesses of our culture. I want to give them a desire to strip life to its essentials and the courage to embrace whatever they find there.

I would teach them to be seers, to notice subtleties in nature, in people, and in relationships. I long for them to grasp the *meanings* of things, to hear the sermons of the seasons, and the exhortations of the universe, the warnings of the wounded environment. *I would teach them to listen.* It would bring me joy to happen in on them one day and find them with their ears to the earth or humming the melody of the meadow or dancing to the music of the exploding symphony of spring.

Yes, I would teach them to dance! I would teach them to never so tie up their feet with the shackles of responsibility that they can't whirl to the rhythm of the spheres. I would have them embrace the lonely, sweep children into their arms, give wings to the aged, and dance across the barriers of circumstance buoyed by humor and imagination into the ecstasy of joy. I would teach them to dance!

I would teach our children to cry, to feel the pain that shatters the violated, to sense the emptiness of the deserted, to hear the plaintive call of the disoriented and lost, to understand the hopelessness of the powerless. I would teach them to cry—for what is locked away, for that which is broken, for those who never knew Life, for what was not realized, for the least, and for those who have never known freedom.

I would teach our children gratitude. I would have them know the gift of where they've been and who brought them to where they are. I would teach them to write each day a liturgy of praise to read to the setting sun. I would have them dwell on the gift of what is, not wasting their energies on what could have been. I would have them know that twin of gratitude, contentment—contented to live and breathe, contented to love and be loved, contented to have shelter and sustenance, contented to know wonder, contented to be able to think and feel and see. To always call a halt to senseless striving, this I would teach our children.

I would teach our children integrity, to be truthful at any cost, to be bound by their word, to make honest judgments even against themselves, to be just, to have pure motives. I would have them realize that they're accountable individually to God alone and, then, to themselves. I would have them choose right even if it is not popular or understood, even by me.

I would teach our children to pray, knowing that in our relationship with God there is much to be said, and God is the One who must say it. I would have them know the difference between prayer and piety; I would make them aware that prayer often has no words but only an open, vulnerable access to God's love, mercy, grace, and justice. I would hope that they discover that prayer brings and is an awareness of our need, a knowledge without which there is no growth or becoming. I would have our children know through experience and example that there is nothing too insignificant to lay before God. Yet, in that openness, we often find Him lifting us above what we brought to Him, making it insignificant compared to the revelation He brings to us.

I would not have our children think of prayer as a commercial enterprise, a sort of celestial clearinghouse for distributing earth's material goods. Rather, I would have prayer teach them that what we so often think we seek is not on the list of what we need. Yet God does not upbraid us for our seeking but delights in our coming to Him, even when we don't understand. Most of all, I would have our children know how synonymous true prayer is with gratitude and contentment and have them discover the marvelous outlet prayer is for communicating this delight with God.

Last, *I would teach our children to soar,* to rise above the common yet find delight in the commonplace, to fly over the distracting disturbances of life yet see from this perspective ways to attack the knotty problems that thwart people's growth and stymie their development. I would give them wings to dream and insight to see beyond the now, and have those wings develop strength from much use so that others may be borne aloft as well when life becomes too weighty for them to bear. At last these wings, I know, will take our children high and away from our reach to places we have together dreamed of, and I will watch and cheer as they fade from my view into vistas grand and new, and I will be glad.

My Heart Would Be Your Bethlehem

My heart would be Your Bethlehem,
A shelter for Your birth;
My body be Your dwelling place,
A sacred temple on this earth.
By holy intervention
An act of the divine,
In union with mortality
Make incarnation mine.

My will would bow in wonderment,
Struck silent by the awe
Of angels' visitation
That wakes my slumb'ring heart, at dawn
With some annunciation
My soul could magnify;
Begin in me a holy seed
That I cannot deny.

My heart, my will, my mind, my all,
I consecrate to bring
The holy Son of God to earth,
Oh, let the angels sing!

My mind would make a pilgrimage
Wherever promise shines,
Illuminate eternal things
That I might not mistake the sign,
No matter what it costs me,
Be journey long or far,
Oh, may I trade all treasure rare
For following Your star.

My heart, my will, my mind, my all,
I consecrate to bring
The holy Son of God to earth,
Oh, let the angels sing!

Lyric: Gloria Gaither
Music: William J. Gaither and J. D. Miller

❦❦❦ *My Heart Would Be Your Bethlehem*

Christmas is personal. It's corporate, too; its varied traditions are celebrated by families, communities, and nationalities. But at the core of the matter, Christmas is personal. For me, perhaps for each of us, Christmas is either an inconvenient outrage or an experience so deeply spiritual that no matter how many impostors—death, divorce, estrangement, loneliness, or broken promises—have violated the holiday itself, there is a deeper thing, a sort of epiphany that converts us year after year from the self-pity of the moment to a "new birth," if you will, of the only Deity who was born weeping for us all.

Over the years, this epiphany has come to me in small moments that illuminate specific details of this deceptively simple-seeming event. Unlike the Santa-centered fable (when you've heard it, you've heard it, and it soon wears out its own credibility), this story of the Incarnation has layers of metaphor that can be enjoyed and appreciated when viewed as a one-dimensional painting or when *entered into,* like walking into a street fair, seeing, touching, smelling, tasting, and listening as you go.

There has hardly been a Christmas, since I was able to perceive Christmas, that hasn't gently pulled me into some soul-shaking insight that has become a part of my life experience and worldview.

If this were not the case, I would not be writing this book, nor would I have written dozens of lyrics about this one singular event in history.

These epiphanies, these small revelations, always come unannounced and largely unbidden. Rather than being pursued, they overtake and capture me while I am intent on some other pursuit of the season: shopping for someone I love, cooking foods that have a history, caring for babies, wrapping something to send away or wedge under our huge live Norway spruce Christmas tree, reading Scriptures I've read a thousand times before, singing in the cold a carol some other songwriter penned long before I was born. However these insights come, I am detoured when it happens, forced to stop, write down a phrase or a verse or an entry in my journal. Sometimes, when I'm speaking for some church service or community or women's event, I hear myself say something I've never read or even thought before. I find my heart stopping to say, *Why, you know, that's true!* as my voice goes on to the next point I've prepared to make.

This song, "My Heart Would Be Your Bethlehem," was a particularly personal thing. It shook me when I wrote it. Evidently, it didn't shake anyone else. When I showed it to Bill, he was sweet but didn't seem overly excited. It sat on the piano for a good long while scribbled on a yellow legal pad.

One day when a young musician named J. D. Miller, from Lexington, Kentucky, was at our house to write music with Bill, this lyric was pulled out and the two of them wrote what we all felt was a good setting for the lyric. To this day, no artist has recorded it, as far as I know.

Yet, when I read it, as I have writing this collection of stories, it moves me, and that is enough. Wrapped in it is a small revelation of how this God-child must be planted in me, how I must be as willing as Mary to bear its ballooning dimensions and face whatever scorn or misunderstanding it may take to carry this inception to its final conclusion. And in the process, I myself will be filled with the wonder of being chosen and bow my heart to worship in awe of something God has caused me to conceive. I, too, not only must journey to the place my personal history charted for me, but I also must not lose touch of the star as I go and I must believe the angels without question. For in analyzing a miracle, one loses its wonder and power to transform. I know, somehow, two things: This birthing of God in me is not just for me, but for others, too; and this birthing is not just for others, but for me as well. In the incubation and delivery process, I, too, will be born, and born, and reborn.

114

The Sender and the Sent

The star that marked the baby's birth was spoken by His voice;
The wisdom of the kings who came was given by this boy;
He wrote the song the angels sang, that echoed through the land;
This Child the girl held in her arms, held the whole world in His hands.

Glory in the highest!
Peace on earth below.
Glory to the lowly,
Yet honest kings may know;
Alpha and Omega,
Throughout time and space He went;
The baby who had always been the Sender and the Sent.

The precious gold they gave to Him He'd first put in the earth,
And in that manger, side by side, lay death as well as birth.
The glorious hosts the shepherds heard, He'd known them from the start;
And the journey down to Bethlehem He'd first made in His heart.

And a Child Shall Lead Them

Lions and lambs, leopards and rams feed together.
Gentle and wild, vicious and mild lie down.
Natures change there at the manger where hist'ry turns the page,
And God breathes the breath of a baby.

And a child shall lead them from their war-torn lands,
Yes, a child shall lead them; they shall go hand in hand.
And My holy mountain shall be filled with peace,
As water covers the ocean, and a child shall lead.

Broken and torn, in silence they mourn a fam'ly,
Shattered, a trust lies in the dust and dies.
Then in that place, wonder and grace, like a seed that sprouts from sand
Remakes a man and a woman.

Lyric: Gloria Gaither
Music: William J. Gaither and Douglas C. Eltzroth

❦❦❦ *And a Child Shall Lead Them*

I have grown up in the church and have heard nearly every theological debate human minds can devise. All through my growing-up years, the various branches of Christendom had it out at my parents' dining room table. Ever since we've had a home of our own, Bill and I have witnessed our share of skirmishes, too. Calvinist, Armenian, Reformed, Covenant, Catholic, Pentecostal, pre-, post-, and amillennial, dispensational . . . *ad infinitum.*

Personally, I think they all are true, but not exclusively so. With Milton, I tend to believe that God is paradox, and we—finite minds that we are—can't abide paradox. We won't be happy until we shove the infinite I AM into some manageable and label-able box called "a systematic theology."

Meanwhile, God manages to leak out through the cracks in our systems and show up in some neighborhood Bible study of young mothers driven together by their hearts, hungry for the Living Water. Oh, my!

One debate I've heard that is way beyond edification is the "literal/symbolic" debate, especially about the prophetic books of the Bible. To this debate, I'm afraid I have to quote Jesus' words roughly translated: "It's not either/or; it's both/and" (see Matthew 23:23). Most disputed issues are debated over the details of a truth so huge that it is able to both embrace our puny human viewpoints and still have plenty of room left over to "confound the wise." Children, of course, get this.

For example, I have heard otherwise intelligent people get really bent out of shape about whether, in heaven, lions, their natural ferocious and carnivorous natures tamed and muzzled by paradise, will actually lie down with lambs.

This miracle would be too small, I think. Unlike hardheaded people, animals already obey the laws of God in nature, and God can change the rules if He wants to. But what a marvel if, here and now, instead of men and women (whose strong wills and natures, lacking love) devouring each other, we would be tamed by the coming of the kingdom "on earth as it is in heaven" (Matthew 6:10 NIV) as Jesus prayed.

What if the "meek lambs" among us could actually lie down in the same field as the aggressive lionhearts among us? What if those of us who are vulnerable lambs could eat (with a calm and trusting spirit) right next to the guy we know is a sure-enough swift, lethal, and destructive leopard—our "natural" enemy.

Could it be that Jesus came for that? Could it be that the angels weren't just humming a holiday tune that night on the Judean hillside when they predicted, "Glory to God in the highest and peace on earth—goodwill to all kinds of people" (see Luke 2:13–14)?

Could it be that this melodic prediction could apply to homes where, instead of being places of peace and balance, it's been more like the Third World War? Could we all be remade by the Savior, this tender plant sprouting from the desert sands foretold by good old Isaiah, this Messiah who would not shout in the streets or break the bruised reeds among us? And aren't we all, on a given day, bruised reeds who don't need a theologian to club us with certainties nearly as much as we need a lover to hold us close?

This child. This Holy Child has come, I'm convinced, not to endorse all the humiliating things that have, sadly, been done in His name through the centuries, but to lead us from the war-torn battlefields of our own making. He has come to cover us with His atonement for all the sick, sad, pointless pain we have caused one another and to heal our land, one broken heart at a time.

And when we're too betrayed and suspicious to trust one another, when utopias turn out to be a facade and politicians who promise solutions prove to be mostly self-serving, when religious institutions are so distracted by their own in-house debates to notice a child slipping off the precipice of society, maybe it will have to be, ironically, a child who will lead us—then grow up to bleed for us so that His immense wounds can, at last, heal us. This is Christmas . . . and Easter . . . and Valentine's Day, too.

Glory in the Highest

Glory in the highest! Glory is His name!
Joy has come into our lives; we'll never be the same.

Glory in the highest! Worthy is our King!
Come let us adore Him, and give Him everything.

Jesus, You have found us when we wandered far,
When we could not find ourselves You came to where we are.

"Glory in the highest!" is more than just a phrase.
Lord, we fall before You now, Your holy name we praise.

Lyric: Gloria Gaither
Music: William J. Gaither, Bill George, and Billy Smiley
Copyright © 1983 by Gaither Music Company, Yellow House Music, and Paragon Music Corp.

Hope of the Ages

Before there was time or space
Or any need for grace,
There was a Word echoing through
The darkness and void.
Grander than what would be,
This Word reached out to me,
Promising Peace,
Promising Hope,
Promising Joy.

    Hope of the Ages,
    Born into time,
    The Word became Jesus,
    Mary's sweet son —
    Savior Divine,
    Promised Messiah,
    A virgin's new boy —

Hope of the Ages,
Glory restored—
Jesus is Joy.

The times were the worst of times.
Violence, war, and crime
Threatened the world,
Made men afraid,
Made mothers mourn.
Then one dark and lonely night,
There came a blinding light,
Splitting the sky—
Angels on high—
A Child is born!

❧❧❧ *Hope of the Ages*

Sometimes songs come in response to a musical style, a form that will then dictate the confines of the idea's expression. This was the case with a piece of music Bill wrote with Ben Speer and Woody Wright; they wanted a Southern gospel convention-style song for the Homecoming choir to sing at an upcoming Christmas videotaping. The project was to be called *Christmas: A Time for Joy,* and a country theme was to flavor the choice of songs.

One of the favorite selections on an earlier Christmas project was an old Southern gospel singing convention–style song called "Beautiful Star of Bethlehem," by two well-known writers of the singing convention era named Adger M. Pace and Fisher Boyce. The song was published by James Vaughan, one of the primary sources for material used in singing convention schools across the South, where the students were taught to sing by a system based on the shapes of notes. In this system, a shape—square, circle, triangle, etc.—represented a tone on the do-re-mi scale. Students who learned this system could easily transpose into any key, since the particular shape always represented the corresponding relative tone on the scale in that key.

"Beautiful Star of Bethlehem" was one of the few Christmas songs made popular by the singing-school convention gatherings, where singers and instrumentalists came to share "dinner on the grounds" and an afternoon of singing.

Bill thought it would be fun to write a current convention-style carol, and I was eager to fit the Christmas story of hope and joy into this well-loved form.

The lyric that came to me after I heard the music the three collaborators had created surprised even me. The historic musical form, introduced into the present, seemed to ask me to take the original historic perspective of the Incarnation story and move it into the present as well.

This promise of hope for which people had waited centuries must have seemed almost impossible to believe. The times were hard. The harsh and ruthless Roman rule was the setting of His coming—rustic and unprivileged. Fear, violence, war, crime—these were a part of every Jew's life in those days.

Fast-forward to the present. War, crime, terrorism, fear—these are no strangers to any of us. Uncertainty, economic challenge, international instability—we hear them discussed on the evening news.

Yet, the promise believers have come to recognize as their hope is not stable economies, crime-free streets, or peace accords. It holds them in the midst of personal and cultural chaos; it bubbles to the surface when things seem at their darkest, and throws a party in their hearts when there is no money for store-bought gifts.

How appropriate that this baby who entered the world so quietly in a stable in Bethlehem would say to us thirty-three years later, as He Himself was walking into the very jaws of terrorism, violence, and murder: "Peace I leave with you, My peace

I give to you; not as the world gives do I give to you. Let not your heart be troubled, neither let it be afraid" (John 14:27 NKJV).

This Christmas, let's all gather around a common table or picnic blanket on the ground, and let's sing for all we're worth! Sing not in unison, but in harmony, each of us taking the part in our range and singing it accurately and enthusiastically. Let's bring the story to this generation and make singing conventions of our circle of families and friends. Invite in the neighborhood and the countryside and pass on not only the song, but the Source of all music:

Hope of the Ages,
Born into time,
The Word became Jesus,
Mary's sweet son —
Savior Divine.
Promised Messiah,
A virgin's new boy—
Hope of the Ages,
Glory restored—
Jesus is Joy!

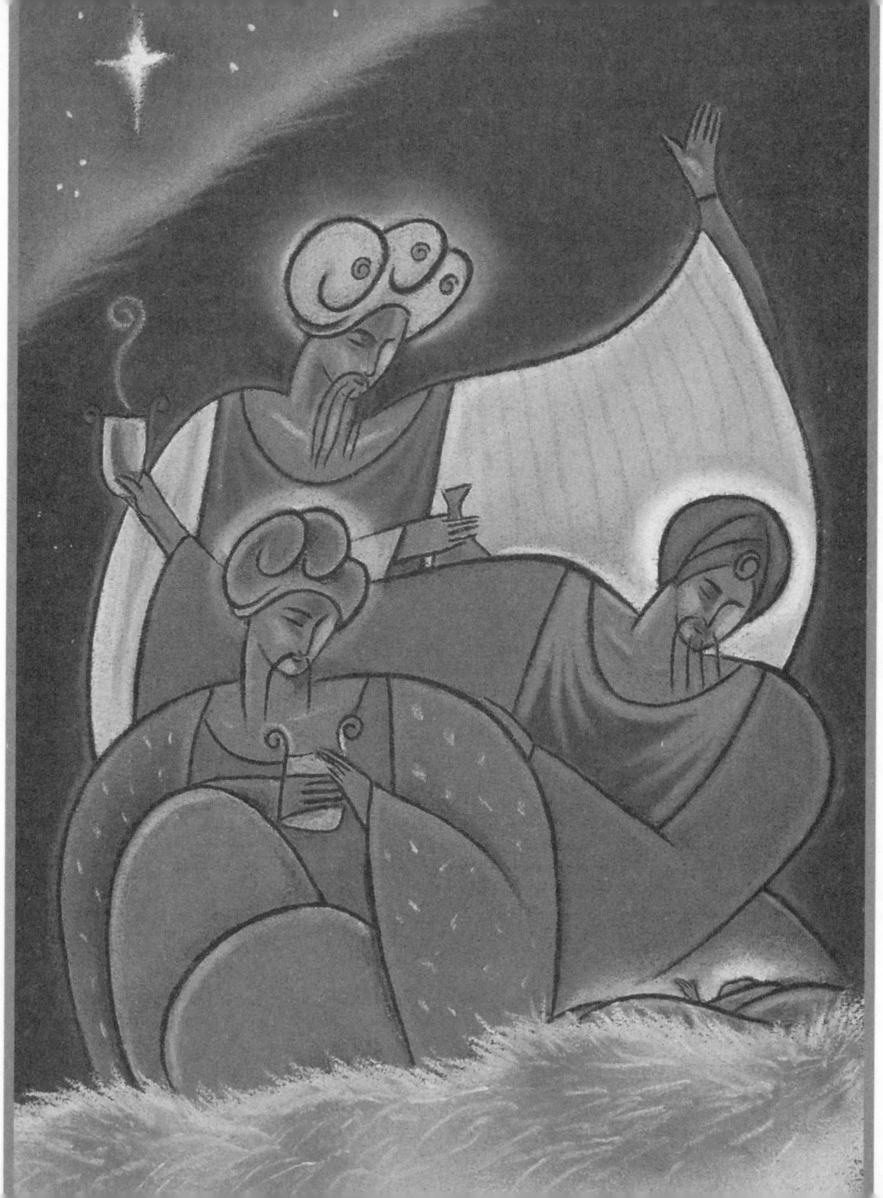

What Did You Say Was the Baby's Name?

What did you say was the Baby's name?
His name is Jesus.
What did you say was the Baby's name?
His name is Jesus.
What did you say was the Baby's name?
His name is Jesus.
King Jesus was that precious Baby's name.

Who was the Baby born in Bethlehem?
His name is Jesus.
Who was the Baby born in Bethlehem?
His name is Jesus.
Who was the Baby born in Bethlehem?
His name is Jesus.
King Jesus was that precious Baby's name.

Who did the shepherds and the wise men seek?
His name is Jesus.
Who did the shepherds and the wise men seek?
His name is Jesus.
Who did the shepherds and the wise men seek?
His name is Jesus.
King Jesus was that precious Baby's name.

Who did they find lying 'neath the star?
His name is Jesus.
Who did they find lying 'neath the star?
His name is Jesus.
Who did they find lying 'neath the star?
His name is Jesus.
King Jesus was that precious Baby's name.

Tell me what did you say? (His name is Jesus)
I love that name
His name is Jesus
King Jesus was that precious Baby's name
What did you say? (His name is Jesus)

I love that name (His name is Jesus)
King Jesus was that precious Baby's name.

King of kings and Lord of lords, His name is Jesus
King of kings and Lord of lords, His name is Jesus
King of kings and Lord of lords, His name is Jesus
King Jesus was that precious Baby's name.

Kings and kingdoms will all pass away,
But His name will live forever,
His name will live forever,
Jesus is that precious Baby's name.

Lyric: William J. Gaither
Music: William J. Gaither

❦❧ *The Right Name*

uliet may have said in the hot passion of youth, "That which we call a rose by any other name would smell as sweet," but Shakespeare knew what she didn't: A name is of vital importance and, as it turned out for Romeo, a matter of life or death.

In one of my favorite books, *Walking on Water* (Shaw, 2000), Madeleine L'Engle makes the point that "to name is to love. To be named is to be loved." The opposite is also true; we all have been diminished by someone who didn't care enough to know us by name.

Wars are possible because human beings are able to exchange names for labels— "those dirty Japs" or "the Krauts" or "those Wops"—and we thus distance ourselves from the fact that all fathers miss their children and all soldiers bleed and every mother groans prayers into the night that her son will come home.

The Bible is full of evidence that God puts a high priority on names. The Scriptures are filled with stories involving names mandated by God. A name is an identity. God's first assignment for Adam was to name every beast and bird the Almighty had formed out of the ground. "Whatever Adam called each living creature, that was its name" (Genesis 2:19 NKJV). God Himself named Adam and Eve, and each of their names had not only meaning but significance.

God also did His share of renaming, calling into existence the hidden, real character of men and women who had been given a name that was too tall or too small for them. The second-born twin of Isaac and Rebekah was named by his parents *Jacob,* the "identity thief." True to that name, he grew up to gain his father's affection by deceiving him into believing he was his brother, Esau, and thereby receiving his blind father's blessing. Yet, because in his soul was a deeper passion to know the divine and secure the approval of God, he ended up in a wrestling match with an angel and was wounded in the struggle. God changed his name from "deceiver-supplanter" to *Israel,* which means "You have struggled with God and with men and have prevailed."

The prophet Isaiah underscored the importance to God of naming when he wrote:

> If each grain of sand on the seashore were numbered and the sum labeled "chosen of God," they'd be numbers still, not names; salvation comes by personal selection. God doesn't count us; he calls us by name. Arithmetic is not his focus. (Romans 9:27–28 The Message)

So the sacred promise to Abraham for descendants that numbered like the stars of the sky and the sands of the sea was redefined through the telescope of the promised Messiah and brought into sharp focus: People may be impressed with quantity, but God sees us one by one and emphasizes the importance of the individual by naming.

Simon the fisherman was renamed by the Lord when he recognized the Christ for who He truly was. "Now I'm going to tell you who you are, *really* are. You are Peter, a rock," Jesus said (Matthew 16:18 THE MESSAGE), and Peter lived the rest of his life redefined.

Saul the Christian-killer got a new identity because of an encounter with ultimate Truth on the road to Damascus. His past forgiven and his misdirected vocation stopped dead in its tracks by a vision of pure light, Saul's values did a 180-degree turn, and a new name began to be used for the changed man who declared he would rather "suffer affliction with the people of God, than to enjoy the pleasures of sin for a season" (Hebrews 11:25 KJV).

No wonder, then, the angels that moved the props and characters into place for the greatest drama the world has ever seen were very careful to carry out the directions of the God who wrote the script when it came to naming the cast.

"His name shall be John," the angel said to old Zachariah. Nine months later, still mute because he had argued with a miracle, Zachariah had learned to stick to the script. When the relatives questioned Elizabeth's choice of a name, objecting that no one in the family had ever been John, Zachariah called for a slate. HIS NAME IS JOHN, he wrote, and with that act he immediately found his voice. (See Luke 1:13, 63.)

Young Mary sat alone in meditation when an angel showed up with a whole series of news flashes for her: A baby would be conceived in her virgin womb by the Holy Spirit; the child would be great and save His people from their sin; by Him would all the nations of the earth be blessed; and *His name was to be called Jesus.* "And so it was, that . . . the days were accomplished that she should be delivered," the ancient story goes, "and she brought forth her firstborn son, and wrapped him in swaddling clothes, and laid him in a manger" (Luke 2:6–7 KJV).

Throughout the accounts of this Jesus' thirty-three years on earth, His name was the cause of both miracles and derision. Just the sound of His name caused demons to flee and children to come to Him. It caused politicians and opportunists to plot His death and thieves and prostitutes to turn honest and pure. At the sound of His name, the poor and the powerless were given dignity and worth, the physically broken were made healthy, and the morally devastated changed into ministers of mercy.

As He walked the dusty roads of His small Middle Eastern homeland, He did His share of renaming people, fitting them with new identities. And I believe it is His intent—this *God with us*—to accurately name us all.

Even though my own parents—probably yours as well—gave a lot of attention to naming, there are days when I wonder who I am, really. I've always known that my name, Gloria, was chosen because my mother believed she was told by God before I was born that God had His hand on my life. I knew, too, that my parents were committed to do whatever it took in prayer, work, or personal sacrifice to help me discover and do what God had in mind for me.

Yet, like every person I've ever met, there are days I struggle with my true identity; I, like you, am most easily hurt by those times when someone who should know me misunderstands my true motives and intentions. Some days I'm a stranger even to myself. Often I still wonder what I will be when I grow up, and see my life as a sort of haphazard attempt at being the true person I know must be buried in me someplace.

Like Mary at the garden of the tomb, I long for Jesus to speak my name in such a way that my life and identity will be suddenly brought into sharp and undeniable focus. So I was overjoyed to discover a great forecast of things to come in the second chapter of Revelation:

> To him who overcomes, I will give some of the hidden manna. I will also give him a white stone with a new name written on it, known only to him who receives it. (2:17 NIV)

Could this be true? I thought to myself. I read it again; I pondered the implications. *After a lifetime search for my true identity, God will give me a white stone with my name on it?* The Scripture seemed to be saying that out of all the stones—all the names—of all the people who have ever lived, I will know immediately that the name on my stone is mine when I see it. It will be a dead-ringer! I will recognize it as the identity I've searched for all my life.

When God names us, the name is accurate. He who alone really knows us will perfectly identify us, and for the first time we will truly be at home in our own skin.

Not only that, God is going to identify His exalted Son. This unspeakable Word will be unmistakably defined:

> I saw heaven standing open and there before me was a white horse, whose rider is called Faithful and True . . . He has a name written on him that no one knows but he himself . . . On his robe and on his thigh he has this name written: KING OF KINGS AND LORD OF LORDS. (Revelation 19:11–12, 16 NIV)

When that name is seen, we do know that "every knee should bow . . . and every tongue confess that Jesus Christ is Lord, to the glory of God the Father" (Philippians 2:10–11 NIV).

Perfect names. Perfect identities. The Shepherd knows His sheep and calls them by name. All the broken, misnamed, misunderstood, unidentified, disenfranchised children of all time will finally be "known." And we shall "know as we are known."

We shall sing a new song, and I believe the new song for us will be the "I AM" He has sung through the ages. At last we will sing: "I am," too.

Jesus, What a Lovely Name

God with us: Common, yet miraculous!
You shall call Him Jesus; It's such a lovely name.
David's throne—Reigning over Jacob's home,
For the Glory now has come, and Jesus is His name.

    Lovely name—
    Jesus what a lovely name—
    All creation now proclaim:
    Jesus! What a lovely name.

Messiah come—healing now at last begun,
Broken Bread to make us one, and Jesus is His name.
Joy restored! While a heart pierced by the sword
Gives birth to a risen Lord, and Jesus is His name.

    Lovely name—
    Jesus what a lovely name—

All creation now proclaim:
Jesus! What a lovely name.

Gaither
Family
Recipes

Almost No-Calorie Vegetable Soup

INGREDIENTS:

- 1 48-ounce can V8 or other vegetable juice
- 1 envelope onion soup mix
- 1 large onion or 3–4 small onions, chopped
- 1 28-ounce can diced tomatoes, including juice
- 1$\frac{1}{2}$ cups coarsely chopped celery
- 1 large sweet pepper (green, yellow, or red), chopped
- 1 head cabbage, chopped (or 1 large bag slaw mix)
- 1 quart water
- Salt and coarse pepper to taste
- $\frac{1}{2}$ teaspoon Tony Chachere's Original Creole Seasoning or Tabasco sauce

Bring all ingredients to a boil in a large soup pot. Reduce heat to medium-low and simmer for at least an hour. Serve with oyster crackers or grated cheese, depending on what diet you are following (low-carb/high-protein–use cheese; low-fat/low-calorie–use crackers).

*

After the indulgence of holiday treats, there is no more delicious and nutritious way to get back into shape than this hot soup. It gets rid of extra water retention, fills the body with nutrients the body can actually use, and is so good you will want a second big bowl. And you can have it!

For a complete meal, serve it over cooked brown or long-grain rice.

Bill's Favorite Apple Delight

INGREDIENTS:

3 cups flour

2 cups sugar

$^1/_2$ teaspoon salt

1 teaspoon cinnamon

2 teaspoons vanilla

2 eggs

$^1/_2$ stick butter

$^1/_2$ cup oil

4 cups chopped apples

1 cup chopped nuts

Mix the first 5 ingredients and then add the remaining ingredients and mix well. Place in a greased 9 x 13-inch pan and add Crumbly Topping below:

CRUMBLY TOPPING:

$^1/_3$ cup brown sugar

$^1/_4$ cup chopped nuts

$^1/_3$ cup rolled oats

2 tablespoons soft or melted butter

Mix well and sprinkle on top. Bake at 350 degrees for 45 minutes.

*

Bill always jokingly says, "It's a good thing the taste of apples and cinnamon isn't a sin; I might be in trouble." And who could resist both when this warm dessert comes out of the oven?

My favorite apple for this all-American treat is the McIntosh that I remember growing in the orchards around my hometown in Michigan when I was a kid. This tart apple with juicy white meat takes to cinnamon and brown sugar like biscuits take to honey.

Our lives are fast-paced and demanding, yet I refuse to give up cooking and filling our home with great smells and warmth. This dessert is quick to make and says, "Welcome home!" in every language. Just add hugs.

A Prayer for Christmas

God, thank You! Thank You for sending Your love right into our world . . . right into our world so we can see it and touch it. Thank You for sending it as a tiny helpless baby so we'd have to touch it and we'd have to hold it close. Your love . . . right where we are.

Thank You, Lord, for Your love that makes us want to reach out to others. Thank You for helping us come to know that love is reaching. Because You love us, we've gained the courage to take the risk of loving. And we've learned that, even when we get hurt, even when we lose, love always wins.

Bill's Favorite Spicy Black Bean Soup

It's meatless and makes a big family-sized potful!

INGREDIENTS:
- 2 pounds dried black beans
- 2 envelopes Lipton's Onion Soup mix
- 1 or 2 large Vidalia onions, chopped
- 1 teaspoon salt (add more to taste after cooking)
- 3 tablespoons olive oil (or more to taste)
- 1 teaspoon Tony Chachere's Original Creole Seasoning (green label) or to taste
- 1 16-ounce jar salsa (mild or medium spicy)

Wash beans in colander with very hot tap water until skins begin to pop open a bit. Place beans and all other ingredients in a large soup pot. Add water to double the depth of beans. Cook on high until water boils; then turn to low and cook for at least 3–4 hours. Add more water, salt, and Tony's if needed. When beans are tender, add one 16-ounce jar of mild or medium salsa.

To SERVE: Spoon a mound of hot cooked rice into large soup bowl, then fill bowl with black beans. Great with corn bread.

The things we remember our grandmothers making in the "good ole days" tasted great, but by today's nutritional standards they had a lot of fats and seasonings we now know we should avoid. This version of a Cuban comfort food has no reasons to avoid and lots of reasons to serve often. Rich in fiber and protein, black beans are delicious and full of nutrition. This recipe, made with olive oil, chopped onions, and salsa, has no animal fat or hydrogenated oils yet is as delicious as you remember Mama's to be.

I make a big pot of this, serve a big salad, make croissants or coffee-can wheat bread, and invite all the kids. I often make it on karate or music lesson night to help my daughters with their heavy schedules.

Brussels Sprouts and Pearl Onions

INGREDIENTS:

1 large bag frozen brussels sprouts
1 bag frozen pearl onions
Salt and pepper
$^1/_4$ stick butter
1 8-ounce container sour cream
Slivered almonds (optional)

Cook large bag of frozen brussels sprouts and 1 bag of frozen pearl onions in a saucepan with just a bit of water until tender. Drain excess water, then salt and pepper to taste. Add butter and sour cream and fold in gently. Serve immediately sprinkled with slivered almonds.

*

I discovered a recipe something like this one years ago in somebody's Thanksgiving ideas and tried it for our big family gathering. To my delight it converted some of the "I-don't-like-brussels-sprouts" part of the family to this great antioxidant vegetable, and I've been making it for special days ever since.

I have found, too, that if I sprinkle chicken bouillon granules in the water when I boil the brussels sprouts, the chicken broth makes them even more flavorful.

Back from Bethlehem

On our way back from Bethlehem
we could have been waylaid by Herods
or stopped down by cynics
who'd say stars are voodoo
and shepherds are ignorant
and there is no breeding
in small towns like Nazareth.

We could have avoided
the tales and the rumors
that swarmed through the travelers—
after all, they were Jewish
and we were all scholars
and could have discounted
parochial legends.

But warnings weren't rumors
and angels aren't legends—

the baby was real as real can be.
And sometimes you just can't
let simplicity throw you—
greatness and riches aren't
always the same.

So, we trusted the warning
and went by our instincts,
turned west and not east, then
circled around, avoided an ambush—
we later discovered—
and went home rejoicing
at what we had found.

Gloria's Perfect-Every-Time Biscuits

IN A LARGE MIXING BOWL:
    2 cups flour
    4 teaspoons baking powder
    1 1/2 teaspoons salt

Work in 1/2 cup shortening (I use butter-flavored Crisco). Break 1 egg into a cup and fill the rest of the cup with milk.

Pour milk and egg into flour and shortening mixture and mix until all ingredients are just blended. Don't overmix.

Pour onto a floured cutting board and gently shape with floured hands until dough is about 1 inch thick. Cut with biscuit cutter and place biscuits in a greased 9-inch cake pan. Keep gently tucking edges of remaining dough into shape but don't handle any more than needed.

Bake biscuits in oven at 350 degrees until lightly golden brown. Serve hot with butter and honey or with chipped beef or sausage gravy.

Chipped Beef and Gravy

INGREDIENTS:

2 4$^1/_2$-ounce jars dried beef (I use Armour packed in a glass jar)
$^1/_4$ stick butter
1 cup scalding hot water
Pepper
2 heaping tablespoons flour
2 cups milk

With kitchen shears cut the beef into narrow strips and place in a large skillet. Add butter and water. Bring to a boil, cover, and reduce heat to a simmer for 10 minutes to coax the flavor from the meat. Add pepper.

Meanwhile, put flour and milk in a shaker and shake until smooth. Gradually add flour mixture to meat mixture over medium heat, stirring constantly. Have extra milk on hand to thin if gravy thickens beyond the consistency of a creamy sauce. Add more pepper if desired (you are not likely to need salt as the dried beef is salty). Serve in a Christmas tureen with stacks of hot homemade biscuits.

*

The only time of the year I make chipped dried beef gravy and biscuits is Christmas morning. The whole family crowds around our big oak table by the kitchen fire (which Bill keeps burning all night Christmas Eve), and there is much happy conversation and storytelling. With the gravy and biscuits I usually serve fresh fruit (berries, melon, mandarin oranges, and bananas) in glasses I've chilled in the freezer, and a big plate of scrambled eggs sprinkled with grated cheddar.

When the children were home, this breakfast followed the reading of the Christmas story from Luke 2 and the opening of gifts, but now that they have Christmas presents in their own homes early, they all come over afterward for breakfast around 10:00. The children bring favorite things to show us, and the conversation is about the great things that happened in their own houses when they awoke on Christmas morning.

After breakfast, we gather in the living room with our last cup of coffee or glass of juice and open presents for one another and the friends we've added and, thankfully, great-grandparents and cousins who still drop by.

Here is what our sweet daughter Amy, now a mother of three, wrote about Christmas morning:

> We're learning that even though traditions are important to us, the fact of the matter is, life changes. And people change; people die and the house we used to do things in isn't there anymore, and the people who used to cook are gone now, or can't

cook anymore. Some of us have moved away, and we're starting our own traditions with our own families. So maybe we can't all be together on Christmas morning like when we were little. Things do change, and guess what—the world doesn't fall apart. And not only that—it turns out that Christmas is very portable! You can take it with you wherever you are. It doesn't have to be "the way it's always been" to be wonderful.

But I don't feel panicked anymore about the thought of everything changing. God has given me such a peace about it all. The important things are still intact. Our connections to one another haven't lessened; in fact, they've strengthened. So wherever Christmas is this year, and whatever it looks like, I know it will be all right. The traditions will still be alive, whether we get to practice them all together or not. And it'll still be Christmas.

(Although I'm really going to be bummed if I don't get to have Mom's chipped beef and gravy with homemade biscuits—I've been craving that all year!)

To Elizabeth

On the way to Elizabeth—
shaky with promise
and questions I knew
she would never demand
that I give her the answers
for I *was* an answer
to questions she harbored—
I traveled in silence.
The silence was pregnant
with anticipation—
Elizabeth, wise
like a mother to me,
would give confirmation
allow all my questions
or embrace the strange silence
and just take my hand—
love me and hold me
or just let me be.

The Word that I brought her
defied explanation,
and all that I knew
was that God was in me.

Clela's Oatmeal Cookies

※※※※※※※※※※※※※※※※※※※※※※※※※※

This recipe came from a dear lady in my parents' church in Burlington, Michigan. It was the *best* and first cookie I ever learned to make.

INGREDIENTS:

- 1 cup soft shortening
- 1 cup white sugar
- 1 cup brown sugar
- 2 eggs
- 1 teaspoon vanilla
- 2 cups flour
- 1 teaspoon each: salt, baking powder, and baking soda
- 1 individual cup serving applesauce or 1 large jar of junior baby food applesauce
- 1 cup raisins (optional)
- 3 cups rolled oats

In large mixing bowl, cream together shortening, sugars, eggs, and vanilla. In another bowl, mix flour, salt, baking powder, and soda. Add dry mixture slowly to egg, sugar, and shortening mixture. Mix well.

Add applesauce and 1 cup raisins. With heavy spoon or by hand, mix in 3 cups oatmeal until well blended. Drop balls of cookie dough onto greased cookie sheet. Bake for 10 minutes at 375 degrees. Cool and store in sealed plastic container to keep moist and chewy.

*

Food in families is a sort of journal kept through the years. My children's children will not have known Clela, but I love it that this tall sprite of a woman, who came to love God during the time my parents pastored in the tiny farm community of Burlington, Michigan, will touch their lives in tangible ways—like in these oatmeal cookies. And maybe some of her delight in life and exuberant and sometime reckless love for God will touch them, too, because her enthusiasm so affected their grandmother.

I've added applesauce to her recipe; maybe my daughters or son will add some ingredient *they* discover, and as we all sit around the fire on cold winter days after school, having had fresh-from-the-oven oatmeal cookies and milk, we'll tell the stories that tie us all to a bigger Story, and the love of God will become so real to those kids they can taste it.

❦❦❦ *From Angel Tree to Angels*

One of the best Christmas celebrations for our family has been to take part in Prison Fellowship's Angel Tree program. We choose a child, sometimes two or three children, whose parents are in prison. Together we shop for the things the child needs. In the past, our children have gone with Bill and me to deliver the presents; this adventure became a tradition in our family.

Now our children are grown and have kids of their own and they are choosing Angel Tree children. Several seasons ago, our son, Benjy, went with me into a very rough neighborhood to deliver the presents. As we drove up in front of the home, we could see someone pulling back the curtain, peeking out the window. They seemed to be apprehensive about strangers in their neighborhood and were hesitant to open the door.

We knocked on the door and stood for several minutes on the porch. Finally, the door opened a crack and a young, single mother peered at me from inside. "We're here to bring presents to your children," I told her. "May we bring them in?" The door opened a bit wider and I could see children watching us from the room behind her. We went back to the car and began bringing in the presents.

A young boy about eleven or twelve years old ran out behind me, yelling, "Is that from my daddy? Is that from my daddy?" "Yes. This is from your father," we told him. A big smile spread across his face.

I can't explain the joy we felt to be part of showing this family that they had been specifically remembered at Christmas. But just as important was what my son and I experienced together, knowing that while we were actually touching this family in this neighborhood, others were working with their imprisoned husband and father, letting him know that God had sent the gift of His Son to truly set him free.

Gaither Welcome Wassail

IN A 32-CUP PERCOLATOR, MIX THE FOLLOWING INGREDIENTS:
- 1 gallon apple cider
- 1 32-ounce bottle cranberry juice

IN PERCOLATOR BASKET, PLACE:
- ½ lemon, scored and cut into pieces
- 6–8 cinnamon sticks
- 10–12 whole cloves
- 6–8 whole allspice
- Optional: 1 teaspoon rum flavoring

Plug in and perk as usual. Serve with a cinnamon stick in each cup.

*

Nothing smells better when guests walk in out of the December cold than the smell of apple cider and spices perking in the kitchen. And nothing tastes so "welcome" as a sip of steaming wassail from a glass mug with a cinnamon stick floating on the top.

I make this recipe in my big thirty-six-cup silver percolator and a houseful of company can return again and again for refills all evening. The kids love it, too, after an afternoon of sledding on the hillside or ice-skating on the pond.

Gloria's Coffee-Can Honey Wheat Bread

IN A LARGE BOWL:

$^{1}/_{2}$ cup warm water

1 teaspoon sugar

1 package dry yeast

$^{1}/_{8}$ teaspoon ginger

NEXT, ADD:

2 tablespoons vegetable oil

2 tablespoons honey

1 15-ounce can condensed milk

MIX:

1 cup whole wheat flour

1 cup unbleached white flour

Add most of flour mixture using electric mixer, then work in the final cup of flour by hand.

Grease two 1-pound or one 2-pound coffee can, including plastic lids. Make sure they're well greased. Drop batter in and seal cans with lids. Let rise until lid pops off. Bake without lids at 325–350 degrees for 30–40 minutes or until golden brown.

Let cool slightly before removing bread from cans. Serve hot with real butter and honey.

*

More and more, I like making things myself to assure that my family isn't getting a bunch of chemicals, preservatives, and additives on top of the already unavoidable toxins in our environment.

This incredible bread is easy to make, and I use organic unbleached and whole wheat flours and honey to make it. It doesn't have to be kneaded and coaxed, either. Just put the dough in a "greased" coffee can (two 1-pound cans are my favorite size, but you could use one 2-pound can). Grease the lid and put it on the can. Let the dough rise in a warm place until the lid pops off. No guessing! Then bake. Be prepared, though: This bread may not last long enough to make it to the table. A little real butter and a dribble of honey or sorghum, and heaven can't be closer while you're still alive!

A Prayer for Christmas

Lord, thank You for my mind. Thank You for the marvelous gift of thought and reason. Lord, I'm sorry; forgive me for all those times when I've used this wonderful gift to question Your very existence.

Thank You, Lord, for speaking to me so intimately through Your Word. It wasn't always this way; until I really came to know You, I thought the Scriptures were only rules, restrictions. Now those very same words say to me in a hundred ways, "I love you. I'm caring about you. I've planned for you." Thank You, Lord, for Your Word.

Heartwarming Tomato Basil Soup

INGREDIENTS:

- 4 cups (8–10) tomatoes, peeled, cored, and chopped, or 4 cups canned whole tomatoes, crushed
- 4 cups tomato juice or part tomato juice/part chicken stock
- 12–14 washed fresh basil leaves
- 1 cup heavy cream
- $^{1}/_{4}$ pound sweet, unsalted butter
- Salt to taste
- $^{1}/_{4}$ teaspoon cracked black pepper

Combine tomatoes, juice, and/or stock in large saucepan. Simmer 30 minutes. Purée, along with the basil leaves, in small batches in blender or food processor. Return to saucepan and add cream and butter, while stirring, over low heat. Add seasonings. Garnish with basil leaves and serve with your favorite bread.

*

Is there anything better after a long trip—like our Christmas concert tour—than to fill a too-long-empty house with the simple down-home smell of tomato basil soup simmering on the stove? It soothes a tired stomach and warms the body. The subtle hint of basil makes the tomato and cream into a picnic for the senses. Sprinkle shredded cheddar cheese on top and serve with a small basket of oyster crackers and celery and carrots. This is another favorite we serve in the Latté at Gaither Family Resources in Alexandria, our place to stop in the Indiana cornfields for rest and restoration.

Incredible Turkey

INGREDIENTS:
- Turkey
- Butter
- Salt
- Pepper
- 3 or 4 apples
- 3 or 4 onions

Wash entire turkey inside and out. Blot with clean dishtowel. Rub turkey with butter, salt, and pepper inside and out. Into a big bowl, coarsely cut apples and onions into eighths.

Stuff the inside of turkey—front and back—as full as you can. Put 1 tablespoon flour in a clear, large baking bag and shake. Insert turkey into the bag, breast side up. Seal bag and place in a huge disposable aluminum oven pan.

Poke a couple of holes in bag to allow steam to escape. Put in oven that has been preheated to 350 degrees. After 30 minutes of baking, reduce heat to about 275 degrees and cook for 6–8 hours.

(Because I bake such a huge turkey, I put the turkey in the oven at 11:00 at night and go to bed. When I get up, I turn the heat down to about 150 degrees just to keep the turkey warm until everyone arrives.)

Split open bag and slice the turkey, then baste slices in juices as you layer onto serving platter. Garnish with parsley or rosemary and serve. Discard the stuffing after all meat has been removed from carcass.

The steam and flavoring from the onions and apples will give your family the most delicious, moist turkey they've ever tasted.

*

I know there will be dozens of recipes this year and every year for "the perfect turkey." Try them if you wish, but trust me, the easiest, most flavorful, and most moist bird you'll ever taste is not that hard.

Many years ago I discovered this secret: Season the bird well, then stuff (and I mean stuff!) the inside of it with chunked apples and onions, and put it in a clear cooking bag dusted with flour. Put the bagged turkey in a broiler pan, in a slow oven (about 275 degrees), and go to sleep and forget it.

The next morning, the most beautifully brown and juicy turkey will be falling-off-the-bone done and ready to slice and eat. We make a late-night event of "putting on the turkey" at our house. By then the tables are set for Thanksgiving Day, the salads are chilling, the pumpkin pies are cooling, and we're all gathered around the kitchen counter drinking Sleepytime tea and telling stories. Usually our turkey is twenty-five pounds or more, so there's plenty for a day of feasting as all the dear ones gather into our rambling old house to give thanks and pass out the hugs and kisses to all the new babies.

❋❋❋ *My Most Memorable Christmas*

$\mathcal{I}$f everything special, warm, and happy in my formative years could have been consolidated into one word, that word would have been *Christmas*. So, by the time the building blocks of my days had piled themselves into something as formidable as late adolescence, Christmas had a lot to live up to.

Christmas, by then, meant fireplaces and the bustle of a big, excited family complete with aunts, uncles, and cousins. It meant great smells from the kitchen, homemade bread, and cranberries bubbling on the stove, pumpkin pies and turkey. It meant Grandma's cheery voice racing to be the first to holler "Christmas gift!" as we came in the door. It meant real cedar Christmas trees, handmade foil ornaments, and lots of secrets. It meant enfolding in the arms of our great family the lonely or forsaken of our village who had no place to go. It meant all the good and lovely things we said about Christmas being in your heart and the joy being in the giving.

Then came that other year.

There were many things that conspired to bring me to the situation in which I would test all my so glibly accepted theories. Grandma was gone, leaving in my heart a vacuum that wouldn't go away. My sister was married now and had the responsibility of sharing her holidays with her husband's family. The other relatives were far away. After a lifetime of serving in the ministry, Daddy had that year felt directed to resign his flock, with no other pastures in mind, and "wait on the Lord." Since I was away at college, just beginning my first year, I wasn't there when they moved from the parsonage to the tiny cottage at the lake that a concerned businessman had helped them build. Nor was I prepared that winter day for the barrenness that can be found only in resort areas built for summertime fun.

There was no fireplace. There was no bustle of a big excited family. Gone was the sense of tradition and history that only the aged can provide, and gone was the thrill of the immediate future that comes with the breathless anticipation of children.

The dinner was going to be small, just the three of us, and there just wasn't any *ring* in the brave attempt at shouting "Christmas gift!" that Mother made as I came in the door. Daddy suggested that because I'd always loved it, he and I should go to the woods to cut our own tree. I knew that now, of all times, I could not let my disappointment show. I put on my boots and my cheeriest face, and off through the knee-deep snow we trudged into the Michigan woods. My heart was heavy, and I knew Mother was back at the stove fighting back the tears—for all that was not there.

There was a loveliness as the forest lay blanketed in its heavy comforter of snow, but there was not a comforter to wrap around the chill in my heart. Daddy whistled as he chopped the small cedar tree. (He always whistled when there was something bothering him.) As the simple tuneless melody cut through the silent frozen air, I got a hint of the quiet burdens adults carry, and for the first time felt myself on the brink of becoming one. So as I picked up my end of the scraggly, disappointingly small cedar, I also picked up my end of grown-up responsibility.

I felt the times shift. I was no longer a child to be sheltered and cared for and entertained. My folks had put good stuff in me. Now, as I trudged back through the snow, watching the back of my father's head, his breath making smoke signals in the morning air, the weary curve of his shoulders, I vowed to put some good stuff back in their lives.

The day was somehow different after that. We sat around our little table, stringing cranberries and making foil cutouts. This time it was not the activity of a child but sort of a ceremonial tribute to the child I somehow could never again afford to be and to the people who had filled that childhood with such wealth and beauty.

Lela Gaither's Delicious Barbecue Meatballs

MEATBALL INGREDIENTS:

2 pounds hamburger

8 eggs

Cracker crumbs

2 medium onions, chopped finely

1 package tomato-flavored dry cup-of-soup mix

Sage to taste

Mix together and form into small, firm balls. Drop into boiling water and cook until they float to the top. Remove and drain on paper towels. Put in sauce (see recipe below):

SAUCE INGREDIENTS:

1 can Campbell's onion soup

1 can Campbell's tomato soup

2 tablespoons cornstarch

2 cloves garlic, minced

$1/4$ cup cider vinegar

3 tablespoons brown sugar

1 tablespoon Worcestershire sauce
⅛ teaspoon Tabasco sauce

Mix well and simmer until thick and bubbly. Sauce will keep for 1 week. Makes about 75 meatballs.

This sauce is great for chicken or ribs, too. Just boil the chicken or ribs until tender, then put them in the sauce.

*

I love the way recipes gather ingredients and secrets as they are passed along like a Michigan snowball gathers layers of snow as it rolls down the hillside.

These meatballs actually began with my mother. Then while I was making them, I discovered that if I dropped them in a kettle of boiling water to cook, the fat content would be greatly reduced and I could always tell when they were cooked through because they would bob to the surface of the water and float. I also added a few touches to the sauce.

Then Bill's mom, the consummate country cook, finessed the recipe and worked her special magic on both the meatballs and the sauce. Now that she's gone, her granddaughter Becky (our niece) makes them "just like Grandma did" and brings them to family gatherings. They never last long, so I have no idea what they would taste like warmed up for another day, but I have a feeling the longer they stayed in the sauce, the better they'd be!

Mother's Orange Cake

Cut 2 oranges in half, squeeze juice into a bowl, and add $^3/_4$ cup sugar. Stir occasionally. Set aside to use after cake is baked.

GRIND AND SET ASIDE:
   3 orange rind halves
   1 cup raisins
   1 apple

CREAM TOGETHER:
   1 cup sugar
   $^1/_2$ cup shortening

ADD:
   2 eggs
   1 teaspoon soda dissolved in 1 cup buttermilk
   1 teaspoon salt
   2 cups flour
   $^1/_2$ teaspoon nutmeg
   1 teaspoon vanilla

Mix well then fold in ground ingredients and nuts. Bake about 45 minutes at 325 degrees. Use a fork to poke holes in hot cake, then spoon reserved orange syrup over cake in pan while still hot.

Mother's Prune Cake

INGREDIENTS:
  2 cups sifted flour
  1 teaspoon soda
  1 teaspoon cinnamon
  $^1/_2$ teaspoon salt
  $1^1/_2$ cups sugar
  3 eggs
  1 cup oil
  1 teaspoon vanilla
  1 cup buttermilk
  1 cup chopped nuts
  1 cup cooked, seeded, and snipped prunes

Sift together flour, soda, cinnamon, and salt—set aside.

Mix sugar, eggs, oil, vanilla, and buttermilk well. Add flour mixture and mix thoroughly. Fold in nuts and prunes.

Pour into a greased and floured 9 x 13-inch pan. Bake at 325 degrees for 45 minutes to 1 hour. Test for doneness in center.

About 10 minutes before cake is done, mix the following:

Sauce ingredients:
 $^1/_2$ cup butter
 1 cup sugar
 $^1/_2$ cup buttermilk
 $^1/_4$ teaspoon vanilla
 $^1/_2$ teaspoon soda

Bring to a boil, stirring constantly for about 10 minutes.

As soon as cake is removed from oven, spoon sauce over cake and down sides of pan. Make small holes in top of cake with fork and continue spooning sauce until all has been used. Cool.

For variety, try snipped, cooked apricots or dates in place of prunes.

Mother's Soft Molasses Cookies

INGREDIENTS:

> 1 cup natural dark molasses
>
> 1 cup brown sugar (packed down)
>
> 1 cup melted butter
>
> 4 cups flour (just a bit less)
>
> 1 teaspoon each:
>> baking soda, allspice, cinnamon, mace, cloves, nutmeg, ginger, and salt
>
> 1 cup chopped pecans or English walnuts

In mixing bowl, slowly blend molasses, brown sugar, and melted butter. Slowly add just under 4 cups flour and sprinkle in spices; mix. Fold in chopped nuts.

Divide into 3 portions and roll into logs about 2 inches in diameter. Wrap each bag in plastic wrap and chill at least an hour. (You may keep this dough longer.)

Slice the dough into ½-inch-thick sections and bake at 350 degrees. Watch closely not to overbake, approximately 8–10 minutes. Cool and store in sealed plastic container between layers of waxed paper.

Incredible with tea, milk, or good coffee.

*

My mother was a busy woman (pastor's wife, writer, youth leader, artist, and mother), yet it was important to her to create and maintain a warm and welcoming home. Three spicy recipes are still sure to bring back to me dear memories of her and our home: orange cake, her prune cake, and her molasses cookies. All of these she made for us at home and also often gave away as comfort to the grieving or in celebration of a new baby or a special occasion. I remember watching her soak the orange cake with the juice mixture while the cake was still hot; I would inhale the irresistible orange fragrance steaming through the kitchen.

Mother hated dry cakes. Maybe that's why she turned the practical goodness of prunes into a moist delicacy fit to serve the governor (or the president, for that matter!). She loved serving this cake warm with something cold on top like ice cream, real whipped cream, or even with cold milk poured over it in a bowl.

The molasses cookies were for harvesttime or Christmas. Gold boxes layered with cookies between sheets of waxed paper were tied

with gingham ribbon or lace and given as a hostess gift or welcome-to-the-neighborhood present. Sometimes she would fill a Tupperware container with these chewy wonders, tie a fabric strip around the container, and give it to a new parishioner or neighbor with a "keep the container" note.

The taste of molasses of any kind and sorghum in particular reminds me of my dad, who loved sorghum and put it on everything from wheat toast to cottage cheese. To this day I keep a "squirt bottle" of sorghum in the cupboard to put on warm biscuits, homemade wheat bread, or bran muffins.

Tastes are a link to those we love as surely as are songs, phrases, sights, and photo albums. My sister and I are orphans now, but these heartwarming tastes and smells are an embrace from parents now gone that we pass on with real hugs to the children of our children.

Nectar-Soaked Fruitcake

INGREDIENTS:

- 2 eggs, lightly beaten
- 1 jar (27-ounce) Borden's None Such Mincemeat with Brandy
- 1 1/3 cups (one 15-ounce can) sweetened condensed milk (like Eagle Brand)
- 1 cup candied red cherries
- 1/2 cup candied green cherries
- 1/2 cup candied pineapple chunks
- 1 cup broken walnuts or pecans
- 1 teaspoon baking soda
- 2 1/2 cups flour

Grease and dust with flour one 9-inch tube pan, two regular-sized bread pans, or four small loaf pans.

Combine eggs, mincemeat, sweetened condensed milk, fruit, and nuts. Fold in dry ingredients. Divide into pans. Garnish tops of cake with half slices of candied pineapple, whole red and green candied cherries, and halves of walnuts or pecans. Bake in slow oven at 300 degrees (2 hours for tube pan; about 1 hour for large bread pans; about 40 minutes for smaller loaf pans). Check centers with a baking test stick. When stick comes out without wet dough, remove from oven.

Nectar for Fruitcakes
> INGREDIENTS:
>> $^3/_4$ cup white Karo syrup
>> 2 cups apricot nectar
>> $^1/_4$ cup rum or brandy (if desired)

While cakes are baking, heat Karo syrup and apricot nectar in a saucepan until just ready to boil. Add rum or brandy and turn off heat and cover. When cakes are done, using a meat fork, poke holes in cakes and spoon nectar over cakes, allowing the liquid to soak in. Continue until cakes have absorbed liquid and surfaces are glazed. Let cool in pans. When cool, turn each cake upside down on heavy plastic wrap; wrap and seal. Then wrap in foil and store in refrigerator for up to 3 weeks. For giving as a gift, tie with Christmas ribbon and tag with handmade greetings; to serve at home just slice and serve with tea or coffee.

*

There is nothing more nostalgic or traditional at Christmas than fruitcake or plum pudding. The trouble is, most people don't really *like* fruitcake. They say it's dry or it's too bitter with citron. I kept experimenting with ingredients and various combinations from recipes until I came up with this incredibly moist, delicious, and beautiful fruitcake. For starters, there isn't much cake—it's all fruit (no citron), nuts, and yummy goo. And, to top that off, it's *soaked* with an elixir that only makes it grow more flavorful when kept wrapped in the refrigerator for two weeks or more.

So I make fruitcakes early in December before things get too hectic, and when some dear friends drop by unexpectedly or I run into my beautician, Bill's barber, or the UPS man (who are all old friends, too, by now), I have something to give that is from our own kitchen yet fit for the most elegant party.

Of course, I have to hide these cakes in the refrigerator behind the loaves of wheat bread, cartons of brown eggs, and bags of fresh produce and grapes. If I don't, Bill finds them in the night and whittles away at them "just a sliver" at a time. So I keep a couple where he can find them and bury the rest behind things.

Pecan Puffs

Beautiful for gifts at Christmas

INGREDIENTS:

1 cup shortening

1½ cups confectioners' sugar (reserve 1 cup for rolling cookies)

1 teaspoon vanilla

2½ cups flour

½ teaspoon salt

¼ cup finely chopped pecans

Cream shortening and ½ cup confectioners' sugar. Add vanilla. Mix flour and salt, then stir into mixture. Add pecans and mix well. Shape dough into 1-inch balls; place on greased cookie sheet and bake at 375 degrees for 12 minutes. Roll hot cookies in remaining confectioners' sugar. Re-roll cookies after they are cool, if desired.

*

These round treats literally melt in your mouth. They are beautiful to serve and a temptation to "sneak" from a cookie jar. The secret is to roll them in powdered sugar once while they are still warm and then again when they're cool. No wonder some people call them Mexican wedding cakes! Of all the treats I make at Christmas, these and the fruitcakes are Bill's favorite.

A Prayer for Christmas

Lord, I'm thankful that Your love has always been driven to create. Thank You for finding so many ways to express Your love in our world. Thank You for color, the russets and browns of harvesttime. The gentle shades of spring, the deep cool greens of the forest, and the subtle tones of the desert. Thank You for texture, the ruggedness of rocks, the softness of a baby's skin. Thank You for the fragrance of the earth. The pungent pine and the delicate lilac, the beckoning smells of the sea. But keep us aware, Lord, that these are expressions of Your love, and that it's You reaching, speaking to us.

Pumpkin Pie

FILLING INGREDIENTS:

Makes filling for two 9-inch pies

> 2 cups pumpkin soup
> 1½ cups sugar
> 3 eggs
> 2 cups *unsweetened* condensed milk (Pet or Carnation)
> 1 teaspoon each: salt, ginger, allspice, cloves
> 1 heaping tablespoon flour

With electric mixer, combine pumpkin, sugar, eggs, and condensed milk. Add spices to flour and mix with a fork. Sprinkle flour mixture slowly into pumpkin batter as you mix to prevent lumps.

Pour into 2 baked 9-inch pie shells (recipe follows). Bake at 370 degrees until center of filling is no longer liquid.

Pie Crust—Perfect and Light
Makes 2 single-crust pies or 1 double-crust pie

Ingredients:
2 cups flour
$^1/_2$ teaspoon salt
$^1/_2$ cup + 2 tablespoons vegetable oil
$^1/_2$ cup + 2 tablespoons whole milk

Mix flour and salt in an ample bowl. Stir in vegetable oil and milk.

Mix with clean hands until flour is evenly mixed in. Do not handle more than necessary. Divide dough in half and shape into a ball; press on a sheet of waxed paper, then cover with another sheet of waxed paper. Roll with a rolling pin until dough is just larger than needed to cover pie pan. Puncture bottom of crust with a fork in a few places, then shape the edges and cut remaining dough from edges with a knife.

Repeat for second pie crust. Fill and bake.

*

Garrison Keillor, a lover of rhubarb pie, once said that the *best* pumpkin pie he ever tasted was not that much different from the *worst* pumpkin pie he ever tasted. But I beg to differ with him. I believe the secret is to not use too much pumpkin in order to keep the custard part as delicate as possible.

Mother gave me this recipe for the filling, and the pie crust recipe was Lela's (Bill's mom). Together they make a perfect pumpkin pie—delicious warm or chilled. We never have a Thanksgiving dinner without it, and now Amy (our daughter) makes it as well as I do.

*

I guess every pie maker has his or her favorite way to make a crust: with lard, with ice, with Crisco, with chilled flour, *ad infinitum.* Most recipes overwhelmed me because there was always some nebulous reason my crust was too tough or too soggy or too something. Then Lela taught me to use this simple foolproof (I needed that!) way to make perfect melt-in-your-mouth crust every time. She said, too, that this crust was so "short" (which means flaky and tender), it was easiest to roll it with a rolling pin between two layers of waxed paper. Peel off the top layer, she told me, and then turn the crust over and center it in the pie pan; then peel off the other layer. Voilà! Perfect. She was right! Then she showed me how to tuck the extra crust under around the edges of the pan and make a lovely trim by shoving the thumb of one hand between two fingers of the other hand, ruffling the pie crust as I go. Of course, I can't explain this in words. That's why cooks teach one another and why families are tied together in the kitchen.

Red Raspberry Cake and Icing

This cake is the number one favorite around the Gaither home. It has been served for nearly every birthday since our kids were little and is now a favorite of our grand-children.

CAKE INGREDIENTS:
- 1 white cake mix
- 3 tablespoons flour
- 1 small package raspberry Jell-O
- 1 cup cooking oil
- 1/2 cup cold water
- 4 eggs
- 1 10-ounce package frozen red raspberries

Mix dry ingredients. Add oil, water, and eggs (1 at a time). Don't overbeat. Break up half a package of frozen raspberries (save other half for icing) and add to batter. Bake at 350 degrees until golden. For best results, use three 8-inch cake pans.

Icing ingredients:
    1 stick butter
    1 pound powdered sugar
    $^1/_2$ package thawed red raspberries

Mix with mixer until smooth. Spread over each layer and then the whole cake.

*

There has hardly been a birthday in this family in thirty-five years that wasn't celebrated with this lip-lickin' cake! When Suzanne was born so near Christmas (December 15), we wanted to make sure her birthday didn't get lost in the shuffle of the holidays. This deliciously pink cake didn't look or taste like Christmas. In fact, it tastes like a stroll down to the raspberry patch.

Let me know how you like it. It has become such a tradition in our family that Suzanne even had the baker make the recipe for her wedding cake. Now a new generation of bakers are making it for birthdays and special celebrations. We even serve it in the Latté Gourmet Coffee Bar at Gaither Family Resources in Alexandria, Indiana.

The Chocolate Cure

This scrumptious treat is sure to be a favorite for all chocolate lovers.

INGREDIENTS:
    1 box regular-sized chocolate pudding (not instant)
    2 cups milk
    1 box devil's food cake mix
    1 package chocolate chips
    $1/2$ cup pecan or walnut pieces (if desired)

Preheat oven to 350 degrees. Mix pudding and milk as directed, and cook until it starts to thicken. Add the dry cake mix and stir until blended. Add the chocolate chips and nuts. Pour into a greased 9 x 13-inch pan and bake for 35 minutes. May be iced with canned chocolate frosting while still warm (I use half a can), or served warm with a dollop of whipped cream.

*

We have a lot of unexpected and unplanned parties. And we love for people to feel welcome to drop in, especially our three, their spouses and children. Bill often brings home friends from the music business who stop by our office, and when that office is "forty miles out of your way on the way to anywhere," as he often says, it's good to find some warm Indiana hospitality.

This dessert is so easy, I can literally make it while guests are gathering their things and getting settled in one of the upstairs bedrooms, or while they warm themselves by the kitchen fire. If you're a baker, you will do a double take when you read the recipe; it sounds as if it wouldn't work. But trust me, this is so easy and so irresistible, you will make it again and again. Serve it hot from the oven with a bit of whipped cream or vanilla ice cream and a steaming cup of coffee or Earl Grey tea.

What does it cure? Everything from loneliness to the "blues."

A Prayer for Christmas

Jesus, Your world is so lovely, but my world is noisy and confused and crazy. I thank You, Lord, that right in the middle of all this chaos, You've touched my life with Your peace. I just want to tell You, Jesus, I love You for being so good to me.

About the Author

Gloria Gaither has authored many books, including such bestsellers as *Let's Hide the Word* and *Let's Make a Memory* (both co-authored with Shirley Dobson), *What My Parents Did Right, We Have This Moment* (pieces from a decade of Gloria's personal journal), *Decisions, Fully Alive, Because He Lives, Friends Through Thick and Thin, Confessions of Four Friends Through Thick and Thin,* The "Blessing" series, *God Gave the Song,* and many publications for children, including the children's series *My Father's Angels, Ordinary Baby,* and *I Am a Promise.* She also wrote the Let's Make a Memory series with Shirley Dobson, which includes *Making Ordinary Days Extraordinary, Creating Family Traditions,* and *Celebrating Special Times with Special People.*

Gloria has written the lyrics for over six hundred songs, including such Gospel classics as "Because He Lives," "The King Is Coming," "Something About That Name," "Something Beautiful," "Upon This Rock," "These Are They," "Let's Just Praise the Lord," "I Am a Promise." She has written a dozen musicals, including *Alleluia: A Praise Gathering, His Love . . . Reaching, Kids Under Construction, In the Gardens, He Started the Whole World Singing,*

Then Came the Morning, and has produced the Homecoming Kids Video Series for children, entitled "The Branch Office."

With the Gaither Trio, Gloria has recorded over sixty albums, some of which have won Grammy Awards. She is the lyricist of over twenty songs that have received the Gospel Music Association's Dove Award and has been named Honorary Doctor of Humane Letters from six colleges and universities, including her alma mater. She has served on the board of directors for the Coalition for Christian Colleges and Universities.

A Note from Bill

A few words about the enclosed CD . . .

During the Christmas holiday there is a lot of hustle and bustle to keep our minds occupied, but around the 15th . . . or the 19th . . . or the 24th . . . things begin to slow down and we look into the eyes of those we love and reflect. It is the one holiday when commerce and activity eventually slows down and we really have time to think; and some of the memories that surface during this time are a little bittersweet for many of us. We begin to remember earlier years, we miss those who are no longer with us, and as the years wind down we sense the passing of time more keenly than at other times of the year.

So when we started writing Christmas songs years ago, I wanted to emphasize the hope that surrounds this season. After all, this is the Hope of the Ages we're celebrating! As we wrote, we caught a fresh glimpse at the joy He brought to earth, and it hit us that during Christmas nearly everyone sings— even people who don't sing all year long will chime in on familiar Christmas carols. Both literally and figuratively, Jesus' birth really started the whole world singing! That, to us, was an exciting new twist to this timeless story.

Now, so many years after those songs were written, bringing our fellow artists into the studio to record some of these songs again was a powerful reminder of the timelessness of these truths that have shaped our lives for the past sixty years. The most difficult part of the task was the process of narrowing down the song list. Then, after we finally narrowed down the songs, we had to further condense them into a medley format so we could fit them onto the CD. I think the outcome definitely gives you the flavor of the past forty years of our musical documentation of the story of Luke 2; and I think even more importantly, you will get a glimpse of that hope . . . that joy . . . that motivated us to write these songs in the first place.

We recorded the songs in January, when it was, indeed, snowing outside. The celebrations just past were fresh on our hearts as we gathered in Nashville alongside friends with whom we have enjoyed making music so many times. It really did feel a little like Christmas Eve with family around the piano as we reflected on the Hope of the Ages together. A few of the voices you will hear on the CD include: Joyce Martin-McCollough, Marshall Hall, Wesley Pritchard, Nathan Young and his wife, Suzanne, Amy Rouse, Michael English, Joy Gardner, and Stephen Hill. We hope, no matter what time of year it is when you put this recording into your CD player, that you will get a taste of the Hope that surpasses seasons and the Love that has been reaching for you down through the ages!

—Bill Gaither